THE WORLDWIDE GUIDE TO CHEAP AIRFARES

Cruise by Freighter (Cargo Ship)
Europe, So. America, Australia,
New Zealand

TravLtips
Cruise & Freighter Travel Assn.
Box 580218 - M2
Flushing, N.Y. 11358
(800) 872-8584
($20 yr., $35 2yrs)

Air Tech $ 349 to Europe
                         from West Coast
destination & departure
time must be flexible

Project Management and Design: Lisa Schulz
Editor: Sue White
Copy Editor: Alison Bloomfield
Managing Editor, Australia: Peter Cramer
Marketing Communications: Avantgarde/US

Contributing Writers
Chris Farabee, Miami · Richard Heend, Hong Kong

Researchers
Beth Baron (Chicago), Chris Blunt (Hong Kong), Marcus Colombano (Singapore), Paul Eisenburg (New York), Diane Groce (Bangkok), Chris Linson (Bangkok), Michele Tanenbaum (New York), Allison Tollstam (Singapore), Joris Wiggers (Tokyo)

Editorial Advisory Board
Judy Jewell, Powell's Books · Nic Kontis, Air Brokers International · Peter Manston, *Travel Books Worldwide* · James O'Reilly, *World Travel Watch, Travelers' Tales* · Carl Parkes, *The Southeast Asia Handbook* (Moon)

Thanks to
American Express Travel Related Services · Ian Berry · David Binetti · Ken Blaschke · Baker & Taylor Bookpeople · Dennis Brown · Dave & Rebecca Carrillo · Kate Coleman · Cathy Cutler · Byron Deeter Terry Denny, IATA · Patti Eger · Loris Essary · Karel Fegyl · Nicola Fish · Donna Galassi, Moon Travel Handbooks · Peter Gill · Benjamin Goldsmith · Steven D. Grothe · Larry Habegger · Edward Hasbrouck · Barbara Hoblit · Pat Houdek, OAG · International Air Transport Association · Rachel Joplin · Jupiter Air · Annie Kirk · Hayley Liu · Steve Markowitz · Doug Moshy · New Image Photo · Bill Newlin, Moon Travel Handbooks · Nolo Press · Allen Noren, GNN's Travelers' Center · OAG, Electronic Edition · Kathie Po · Greg Posey · Quality Books · Takeyoshi Sakai · Bob Sanchez · Ron Silverton · SF Net · Tourism Authority of Thailand · Topaz Enterprises · Upper Access Books · United States Department of Transportation · Jason Wallace

Thanks for providing guidance and inspiration
Doug and Kathe McColl · Gert and Betty King

Eternal gratitude to the Project Team
Lisa, Sue, Marcus, and Alison, without whom this book simply could not have been completed.

Insider Publications, 2124 Kittredge Street, Third Floor, Berkeley, CA 94704 USA
Copyright © 1989, 1990, 1992, 1995 by Insider Publications

Printing History:

June 1989	First Edition
December 1989	Second Edition
June 1990	Third Edition
December 1992	Fourth Edition
January 1995	Fifth Edition

ISBN: 0-9633512-1-4
Library of Congress Catalog Card Number: 94-77556

♻ Printed in the United States of America on recycled paper.

THE WORLDWIDE GUIDE TO CHEAP AIRFARES

How to Travel

The World

Without Breaking

The Bank

MICHAEL WM. McCOLL

INSIDER PUBLICATIONS

San Francisco · Sydney

C O N T E N T S

FOREWORD

In the eternal battle between the passenger and the airlines, no arena is more important than airfares. Airfares are also the arena in which the opposing sides are most unequal.

On the one side is the full-time airline Goliath, armed with arbitrary restrictions designed to be failed by those who can afford to pay, sophisticated computer programs constantly repricing the next seat as high as the market will bear, international cartels dedicated to limiting competition and maintaining prices, misleading discount fare ads with the small print missing, commissioned phone operators chirpily guiding you towards the most expensive ticket, and so on.

On the other side, is you, the hapless part-time traveler, who has a vague feeling he is being ripped off, but lacks both the time and the experience to know what to do about it.

The only way you will have any hope of zapping the airline Goliath between the eyes is to fill your sling with knowledge. But finding that knowledge is extremely difficult—mainly because it is either in the hands of the people who want to charge you a high fare or in the hands of people who for one reason or another lack the ability to disseminate it.

That's why a book such as *The Worldwide Guide to Cheap Airfares* is indispensable. A book like this helps you learn how to beat the airlines at their own game—either through manipulating their practices and rules or through by-passing the airlines altogether via consolidators, courier flights and charters.

So if you are interested in raising your status from hapless part-time traveler to invincible fare warrior—start by reading this book. Now.

George Albert Brown
author, *The Airline Passenger's Guerrilla Handbook*

Dear Reader

This book is meant for the adventurous among you. Not for the arm-chair traveler, but for the bold person who wants to get out there and experience the world firsthand. Like me, you're itching to get back on the road, to get another fix of travel and thus ever-so-briefly satisfy your wanderlust.

I embarked upon this project back in 1989, out of frustration. I knew that budget travel opportunities were out there, I just didn't know how to find out about them. Today, information on cheap flights remains elusive. By and large, the companies who have access to cheap airline seats lack the ability to make themselves known. This book exists in order to teach those of you who wish to travel cheap-ly how to do it and whom to contact. It puts the right contact information at your fingertips so that you can quickly and easily reserve a cheap ticket to the destination you choose.

Some of you will remember worker-owned People's Express, a small airline which pioneered low-fare, no-frills flights across the Atlantic in the early 1980's. Their plan was simple: by offering very low fares, they would attract people who never before thought they could afford to travel. People's Express gained quite a following, but overex-tended itself and finally fell victim to bigger competitors. One day, a company like People's Express will make long flights inexpensive again, much as Southwest and its followers have done for short hops. Until then, the secret to flying inexpensively is to use the strategies you have right here in your hands.

But if you want to follow my philosophy, don't stop traveling inex-pensively the moment your plane touches down. Try following your cheap flight with stays at youth hostels or local, family-owned bed and breakfasts. Consider eating at the small, neighborhood places where the waiters still call the chef "Mom." Away from the cultural sterility of corporate-owned hotels and chain restaurants are places where the serendipity of travel flourishes, and where you'll experience chance encounters with the local people. Encourage such moments, and you will understand why I find travel so alluring.

The next time you travel, consider trying out the local dance, or pulling up a stool to chat at the local pub. That home-cooked meal I enjoyed with new friends in the foothills of central Morocco still makes me salivate! Keep in mind that by getting involved with the local people, you can be giving them a memorable experience as well. Maximize your chances for interactions with the people at each place you come upon, and you are bound to become addicted to this kind of travel.

Of course, you do have to get there first. You can travel farther than you dreamed for less than you imagined. The rest of this book shows you how.

FREE OFFER

Let us be perfectly clear here. I want you to travel. That is why I wrote this book, and why you read it. The more often you travel cheaply, the more people will beg you to tell them how you did it, and the more people will hear about this book. So let me make you an offer you can't refuse: use one of the strategies in the book, and take a trip. When you get back, send me a note explaining what you did, and how everything worked out. If I use your comments in the next edition of this book, I'll send you a copy of it for free! So if you travel, you can get two editions of this book, for the price of one.

This free book offer also extends to suggestions about whom I should list in this book. If you are the first to recommend a strategy or company that I later use in the book, I'll send you a free copy of the new edition, too. Send in the first complaint about a company that I drop, get a freebie. I need input from the thousands of readers who use these strategies. People just like you help make this book bigger, better, and more accurate with each new edition.

Send your reports, suggestions, postcards (hint hint), etc. to:

Insider Publications
2124 Kittredge Street, Third Floor
Berkeley, CA 94704 USA

e-mail: insider@sfnet.com

ABOUT THE AUTHOR

Author Michael McColl says, "Budget travel is in my blood!" A graduate of the University of California at Berkeley, he spent his Junior year studying at the University of Barcelona, Spain. He claims to this day that his travels through Europe formed an integral part of his educational experience. Later, Mike returned to Europe to work as a whitewater raft guide in the Catalan Pyrenees.

Mike refined his travel writing the hard way. As one of the founding writers of Fodor's budget travel series *The Berkeley Guides,* he sweated his way through the deserts and industrial factory-towns of northeastern Mexico. (Okay, he snuck in a review of a beach or two here and there, but only when it was absolutely necessary. . . .)

Back in Berkeley, Mike began writing *The Worldwide Guide to Cheap Airfares* in 1989. Between editions, Mike tries to justify traveling as much as possible. Using consolidator tickets, courier flights, and charters, he has traveled extensively through the United States, Europe, North Africa and Latin America. When not on the road researching for the next edition of *The Worldwide Guide to Cheap Airfares*, Mike makes his home in San Francisco, California.

DEMYSTIFYING BUDGET AIRFARE STRATEGIES

Beating the Airlines
at Their Own Game

Travel is an adventure. It is unpredictable, exciting, and above all, mind-opening. Travelers return home refreshed, with new stories, new perspectives, and hopefully a few new friends. Author Rick Steves calls travel "one of the last great sources of legal adventure." Yet for all its benefits, most people find themselves unable to travel as often as they would like to.

The first challenge for most budget travelers is the airfare hurdle. By manipulating their carefully honed computer reservation systems, the airlines do their best to shake as much money as possible out of the consumers' pockets. But you can beat the airlines at their own game. This book will show you how.

Ever notice how you can call an airline three times and get three different prices for the same flight? Airline pricing is a complex, messy process, full of loopholes, quirks and exceptions. Most people (even most airline reservations agents) are baffled by the system. That's why most people end up paying much more than they should. However, once you begin to use the strategies outlined in this book, you can wield the weapons of the airfare market against the very airlines who created the system. I think of it as poetic justice. In trying to take your money, the airlines have made it possible for some of us to pay a lot less.

You will learn how to use discount travel "consolidators" to buy cut-rate tickets for seats the airlines fear they would be unable to sell. You will also read about charter flights, which take advantage of airline price-gouging to sell planeloads of cheap tickets to some of the world's most popular destinations. And you will learn about courier flights, where you get a steeply discounted plane ticket in exchange for carrying time-sensitive documents. When you use these strategies, you will save ten times the cost of this guide the very first time you fly.

Once you have mastered the tricks of the trade, you'll have your chance to apply them to your own globetrotting adventure. We have listed the best providers of cheap travel available in a dozen budget travel hub cities, worldwide. If you live in or near one of these highly trafficked, highly competitive hub cities, you have a whole chapter of cheap travel options just for you. But the hub cities are listed primarily as stepping stones to cheap travel. Use them as jumping-off points, no matter what your initial departure city may be.

If you live far away from our hub cities, just arrange your own transportation to a hub which offers cheap flights to your final destination. It is worth it to get to a hub city—most local travel agencies do not even attempt to compete with consolidator, charter, or courier prices. So instead of flying straight to Africa, consider flying through the ultimate budget travel hub city, London. You are bound to save money, and you'll get the added benefit of staying in the hub city for a day or two, if you choose. We even include a miniguide to each hub city, so that you will have enough information to enjoy a few days there while en route to somewhere else.

THE ECONOMICS OF AIRFARES

When the airlines weave their complicated web of restrictions, classes and fare codes, they have a sensible purpose in mind. They want to extract as much money as possible from the flying public.

Business travelers flying on short notice have been identified as a particularly deep-pocketed and vulnerable market, so they end up getting the worst of the airline price structure. Leisure travelers who plan their vacations months in advance (and have lots of flexibility in terms of when, where, and with which airline they fly) get much better prices. To a great extent, the fare you pay will be determined by who the airline thinks is paying the bill. Business travelers, whose flights are paid for by their companies, will often pay whatever the airlines ask. Leisure travelers are paying out of their own pockets, so they will stay home rather than pay outrageous airfares.

No airline would dare to come right out and say that they are gouging business travelers. Instead, airlines devise all sorts of interesting restrictions, most of which (purely coincidentally, I'm sure) make the cheapest airfares unavailable to business travelers. The theory is that few executives will stay away from home on a Saturday night just to get a cheaper fare.

You can use these restrictions to your advantage. A study reported in

George Albert Brown's *Airline Passenger's Guerrilla Handbook* found that 91 percent of U.S. air travelers paid an average of 40 percent of the full fare for their flights. That means that only nine percent of travelers completely failed to meet the airline restrictions for lower fare tickets. So if you can purchase your tickets far enough in advance, stay over a Saturday night, stay 7 or 14 days on international flights, or fly midweek, you will pay less than full fare. But even if you can't meet the restrictions, there are still cheaper ways to fly.

On international flights, supply and demand often play second fiddle to government regulation. Under the Chicago Convention of 1944, national governments agreed to control fares for flights to or from their countries. Since many national airlines are actually owned by their governments, there is a tendency for the government-approved fares to be high. Worse yet, the governments tend to approve the fares agreed upon by the International Air Transport Association (IATA), which is a cartel made up of most of the world's airlines.

Luckily, the IATA cartel has its weaknesses, which create opportunities for cheap travel. First, IATA has no police power of its own, so it cannot enforce its official fares. Second, many countries look the other way when an airline sells seats at lower-than-official prices. The governments of the United States and Britain, for example, seem to look upon this discounting as a benefit to consumers, so they allow it to continue. In such markets, the airlines use discount travel agents to discreetly unload the seats which the airlines themselves were unable to sell. Technically, the airlines have not sold these tickets, so they can maintain their claim that they never sell seats below the official rate. Third, in countries where the government does scrupulously enforce IATA prices (as is often the case in Europe), a market for charter flights flourishes. Charter operators are not members of IATA, and therefore are not bound to IATA prices. The charter operators undercut the airline prices, and cram their planes full of budget-minded travelers.

Another good source of budget airfares is courier travel. Courier flights take advantage of a loophole in customs regulations, rather than airline restrictions. Because of a quirk in the Geneva Convention, express shipping companies must use a passenger in order to clear their packages through customs as soon as the plane lands. The shipping companies will regularly pay about half of your airfare in exchange for the use of your checked baggage allowance. If you meet the requirements, courier travel is one of the best airfare bargains available today.

In the following sections, the details of discount travel agencies, charters, and courier flights are explained. The pros and cons of each strategy are outlined, as are the most advantageous times to utilize each method. Then we guide you across the globe, stopping at each budget travel hub city to uncover the best airfares available. If your trip starts from a non-hub city, then analyze your route to determine if you might pass through one of the hubs. Not only will you often get a cheaper airfare, but also a pleasant addition to your trip, if you so choose. Be creative in combining routes and strategies—it gives you a huge advantage over the airlines.

CONSOLIDATORS

Consolidators are the "factory outlet stores" of the airline industry. Just as clothing manufacturers sell excess merchandise at out-of-the-way factory outlets, the airlines sell excess seats at out-of-the-way discount travel outlets. Naturally, the airlines are very quiet about this system for discounting tickets. If everyone knew about it, the airlines would find it difficult to sell tickets at their higher, published prices. Nonetheless, savvy travelers have become increasingly aware of this savings opportunity. By using consolidators, you can fly on a major airline without sacrificing convenient scheduling or comfort. You will simply be paying hundreds of dollars less than the person next to you, for the identical flight. Here's how the system works:

The laws of supply and demand say that if the airlines dropped fares to a low enough level, they would sell every single seat. (With the noticeable exception of Southwest Air, the airlines have claimed for years that they could not make a profit at that price level.) Southwest's success notwithstanding, most airlines continue to set fares so high that they almost never sell all the seats. On average, planes are only 66 percent full. That means that one-third of the average plane's seats are empty. This is not profitable.

Consolidators fill those empty seats for the airlines. To understand their role, you must first think of airline seats as a perishable commodity. Each seat has some monetary value to the airline right up to departure time. But if the seat fails to get sold before takeoff, the airline earns nothing for it. Airlines would rather earn some money for a seat than none at all. That's where the consolidators come in.

When an airline worries that some of its seats may "perish" (remain unsold at departure time), it has the option of lowering fares to attract more passengers. However, competing airlines are likely to retaliate with fare cuts of their own. This kind of airfare war is the type of thing that puts airlines into bankruptcy, so they try to avoid it. Instead, the airline often sells its excess seats at a deep discount to airfare consolidators. The consolidators mark up the tickets by about 10 percent, and sell them to retail travel agents and sometimes to the public. The airline receives some money where it otherwise would have gotten nothing, and the passenger gets to fly at a hefty discount.

Also important is how the consolidator market does *not* work. Legend has it that consolidators buy excess seats from the airlines at the last-minute, and then sell them to the public for whatever they can get. This is a myth. Consolidators buy tickets one at a time, as they need them, but at a discounted price. The airlines pay attention to the large trends, and may discount based on those trends (that's why mid-week flights are cheaper), but they never change prices on a single flight because it is about to take off empty.

Consolidators who sell only to other travel agents are called "wholesalers." Consolidators who sell to the public are called "bucket shops," or simply discount travel agents. There is surprisingly little difference in the price for tickets bought directly from a consolidator, and those bought from a bucket shop (who buys from a wholesaler). Frequently, a consolidator has a direct contract with one or two airlines, and uses wholesalers to buy seats on other airlines. For the sake of simplicity, we have listed only the firms who will sell directly to the public, and refer to them all with the term "consolidator." In a few cases, we list agents who deal almost exclusively in consolidated tickets, but do not have direct agreements with the airlines. We refer to these companies as "discount travel agencies."

Like clothing outlets who have to remove the labels, consolidators often are forbidden to advertise the airline's name in conjunction with their deeply discounted fares. However, they will tell you the name of the airline by telephone when you call them. Sometimes the cheapest flights are on little-known airlines. If you feel more comfortable on a name-brand airline, ask the agent. They can often book you on another airline for only a few dollars more.

Consolidators have been called the "illegitimate children" of the airline industry—the airlines created consolidators, yet claim no knowledge of them. But these unrecognized offspring can come up with some amazing deals, even if slightly bending the airline rules here and there.

One consolidator trick is to buy tickets abroad, and import them back to the traveler. Some airlines never discount in their home markets, so to get a good deal you have to look abroad. For instance, Aeroflot categorically discounts all of its fares everywhere in the world, except the former USSR. The best deal for domestic travel in your country might only be available in Dubai! Some consolidators will tell you that this cannot be done, but in reality it is done every day. If you need to import a ticket, look for agents who specialize in around-the-world fares (try San Francisco and London). These agents have contracts with the airlines that give them a great deal of flexibility in constructing fares, which puts them in a good position to export tickets.

Another trick is the "local currency strategy." Where one country's currency is particularly weak against another, very good deals on international flights can be had simply by buying in the right currency. These strategies are often best left to your consolidator, although in the case of Singapore, you can walk across the causeway to Malaysia and see for yourself.

Consolidator tickets are usually as cheap or cheaper than the lowest, advance purchase excursion (APEX) fare available from the airline. It makes sense to shop the airlines first, so you will know how good the consolidator prices are. The downside to consolidators is that if your flight is delayed, you may not be able to use your ticket on another airline. Nonetheless, these tickets are often your best bargain if you haven't planned ahead. If there is any chance that you may need to change or cancel your flight, consider buying trip cancellation insurance.

The safest way to buy a consolidator ticket is through your favorite travel agent. However, the agent may charge you an additional fee, because finding consolidator fares is time-consuming and the commission is low. To maximize savings, price shop at several consolidators.

The bucket shops listed in this guide tend to be established, larger discounters who have built up a good reputation. Smaller, local bucket shops, especially those catering to a particular ethnic group, may have similar or even better deals. If the deal seems too good to be true, call the local Better Business Bureau and check them out. And try to pay for your tickets with a credit card, so you can dispute the charge in the unlikely event that something goes wrong. If you never receive a purchased product, your credit card company will often credit the amount paid back to your account.

As just mentioned, consolidators are often forbidden to advertise the airline's name when offering tickets at these low prices. This makes for a good clue when you're are looking for the latest consolidator flights. Look for their tiny ads, with nothing but destinations and fares listed, in the travel section of your Sunday paper.

CHARTER FLIGHTS

Charter flights are one of the most familiar options for those who seek budget travel. These flights are the "Brand X" of the airline industry—they offer generic airline services for a less-than-brand-name price. And just as your generic corn flakes are sometimes made by one of the leading brands, your charter flight may sometimes be booked on a plane belonging to a major airline.

Charters follow seasonal increases in demand. In the summer, the crowds head to Europe, so the charter operators undercut the regular airline prices and fly thousands of people to Europe. Come wintertime, some people want to ski, while others hope to get away to someplace sunny. The charters then run to the Rocky Mountains or the Alps, and to the Caribbean or the Mediterranean. Whatever the season, the planes are full, so the fares can be lower.

Myths persist about the risks of charter flights. Every once in a while you hear of unscrupulous charter operators who suddenly disappear, leaving passengers stranded at the airport with no way to get a refund. I agree that this has happened before, but for each horror story, hundreds of thousands of passengers have enjoyed perfectly safe and reliable flights. Keep in mind, too, that scheduled airlines can also go out of business. Remember Pan Am and Eastern? As always, pay by credit card so you can dispute the charge if something goes wrong. But if you use the reputable companies listed in this book, you have very little to worry about.

The most important difference between the airlines' scheduled flights and charter flights is a legal one. When you buy a ticket with a major airline, the airline itself is legally bound to provide the services. However, when you fly a charter, your contract is not with the airline, but rather with a "tour operator." A charter tour operator rents a plane (or sections of a plane) from the airline, and then sells seats until the plane is full. If a flight is canceled, requests for refunds must be taken directly to the tour operator.

As hard as it may be to believe, the seating on charter flights can be even less comfortable than economy class on a major airline. However, the charter operators sometimes offer nonstop flights on routes where the major carriers would require a stopover or a connecting flight through the airline's hub city. In general, you should fly charter only when it offers a clear advantage over the scheduled airlines. If a charter fails to offer cheaper fares or a more direct route, then go with the more comfortable seats on a scheduled airline, and buy them at a discount from a consolidator.

Lower prices are the big selling point for charter flights. You usually save 15 to 35 percent off of typical airline fares, and you can save up

---

C H A R T E R   F L I G H T S

P R O S

1 Entire planes full of cheap seats in high season

2 No advance-purchase requirements

3 Often the only nonstop option from a major city to a major tourist destination

C O N S

1 Cramped, "cattle-car" seating, made worse by extremely full planes

2 Very long, tedious check-in lines for many charter flights

3 Irregular flight schedules, including infrequent flights and odd departure times

4 Limited to peak travel times and popular destinations

5 Often one-way flights not available

---

to 50 percent if you book a charter flight on short notice, when there are no discount tickets left on the major airlines. Charter prices offer the greatest savings during high season. Charters may be your best bet if you are headed to ski country, Hawaii, and the Caribbean this winter, or between North America and Europe this summer. Similarly, European travelers will find an abundance of charter fares available from cold northern areas to the beach resorts of Greece and southern Spain.

You can buy seats on a charter flight from most travel agents, although full-fare travel agents are unaccustomed to looking for these flights, and sometimes need to be prodded. Discount travel agents will often offer charter fares in conjunction with their steeply discounted scheduled flights. In fact, some discounters have been criticized for selling charter seats without informing the passenger that it is a charter flight. In my experience this is rare, but if it is important to you, ask. Space-available, or "standby" tickets are often sold on charters, since in order to be profitable, charter operators need to sell almost every seat on the flight.

As with any form of budget travel, the more flexible you are when booking a charter flight, the more money you are likely to save. A charter may not have flights every day of the week. But give them a couple of possible dates, and they are likely to save you a bundle.

THE AIR COURIER PATH TO CHEAP TRAVEL

Carry documents for an international shipping company and save about half of your airfare? It sounds too good to be true. But it happens every day, and has been going on now for about 30 years. Once you have flown as a courier, you may never pay regular over-the-counter fares again.

Courier flights have always had a cult-like popularity among the savviest of travelers. Yet courier travel is now becoming almost mainstream. A recent article in *The Wall Street Journal* reports that travelers can cut the cost of international flights by 50 to 85 percent by taking advantage of courier flights.

When word first got out about air courier flights, insiders worried that their secret gravy train of cheap airfares would be derailed. There were few courier flights available, and increased passenger demand would overwhelm the supply of cheap seats. This was in the mid-eighties. Rather than dying out, courier opportunities have increased dramatically. A flock of new courier firms and brokers sprouted in the late eighties, and the larger companies are still expanding their networks as of mid-1994. Business depends more and more each year on guaranteed overnight shipping, so the need for couriers should do nothing but increase continuously for the foreseeable future.

According to *U.S. News & World Report*, about 25,000 courier flights depart American cities each year. Similar patterns exist in Europe and the Pacific Rim, so the true number of courier opportunities in a given year may approach 100,000 flights. In short, there are plenty of courier flights available for those who know how to sign up for them.

WHAT IS A COURIER?

An air courier is a person who delivers packages for companies that are in the international overnight shipping business. Typically, the courier must give up his checked baggage allowance for the shipping company's mailbags. In exchange, the courier gets a free or discounted air ticket.

WHY DO THE COURIER COMPANIES DO IT?

We've all heard about those international air freight services, the ones that promise to deliver your package to any place in the world, "overnight, guaranteed!" These companies, (Federal Express, DHL, etc.) tend to handle an enormous volume of parcels, especially from one regional center to another. So it is usually cost-effective for them to use their own planes to carry the shipment. But when a company has only a few letters (or at most a couple of mailbags) to send, it is not cost-effective to fly a whole 747 to a distant city. Instead, the shipping service turns the packages over to an air courier company.

Courier companies are the clearinghouses of the express shipping business. They handle the small quantities of overnight freight that the big shipping companies don't want to deal with. Because overnight shipping is in great demand, courier services deliver at least a few items every day to the cities they specialize in.

Commercial airline seats are the cheapest way to move small quantities of freight, quickly. An advance purchase airfare (which allows the passenger to check two pieces of luggage) is relatively inexpensive. On days when there is more than two bags worth of freight, the firm can check the rest as excess baggage, and it will still get on the plane with the passenger. Further, upon arrival in a foreign country, passenger baggage is handled faster than cargo. The edge may only be an hour or two, but that can be the difference between overnight and second-day delivery. Largely for this reason, courier companies reserve airline space every day of the week to each of their destination cities.

Of course, courier companies could still use the freight service that all major airlines provide. But there is another problem. All packages must go through customs at the destination country. Unattended packages tend to languish in a customs warehouse somewhere (sometimes for days), until the local customs officials finally get around to inspecting them. If, however, a package is accompanied through the airport as the luggage of a responsible individual traveler, it clears customs almost immediately.

This is where you and I come in: courier companies need individuals like us to accompany their mailbags through customs. They have to get the packages from Point A to Point B as quickly as possible. In fact, they need us so badly that they willingly pay about half of our airfare! In exchange, they get to use part or all of our checked baggage allowance.

SO WHAT'S THE CATCH?

To get a courier flight, you must first be willing to fly (and return) when the courier company has an available seat. (Of course, the same case is true when you fly on a standard, full-fare airline ticket.) Then, you must be willing to let the courier company use your checked baggage allowance. And you will only find international courier flights, since on domestic flights there are no customs checkpoints through which shippers would need their mailbags accompanied.

What about the clothes and other belongings that you'll want to take with you? It is true that the courier company will generally use your entire checked luggage allowance to transport their mailbags.

However, you get to use your entire carry-on allowance for your personal gear. As a general rule, couriers on flights to or from the United States can bring one bag (weighing less than 20 kilograms, or 44 pounds) to be placed in the overhead compartments, as well as a second bag (length + width + height = less than 45 inches) to be placed under your seat. On other flights, couriers may be restricted to one carry-on bag weighing less than 20 kilograms. This should be plenty of space for the efficient traveler's belongings. And remember, there is no rule about how much clothing you can wear onto the plane. If your bulky sweaters and coats do not fit into your carry-ons, wear them onto the plane. At your seat, peel off the excess layers and put them in the overhead bins, or into a spare nylon bag you just happen to have in your pocket.

To be a courier, you need to be adventurous and flexible. For example, you don't get your ticket until you arrive at the airport meeting point. If you are a worrier, this may not be the best option for you.

While courier travel is usually hassle free, there are occasional foul-ups. Your contact person may not arrive at the meeting point precisely on time. Worse yet, on very rare occasions couriers have been bumped to the next day, or their tickets have gotten to the airport too late. If you are an inflexible, risk-averse traveler, do not fly courier. But I remind you that even the major airlines occasionally cancel flights.

If you do fly courier, bring the local telephone numbers of the courier company with you on your flight, so you can call in if there is a problem. You might even bring the name of the local courier company, written in the local language. Also, remember that the airline employees are very familiar with the whole courier procedure. If you cannot find your contact, ask the people at the airline check-in counter.

HOW DO I KNOW I'M NOT SMUGGLING CONTRABAND?

This is the first question people ask when the subject of courier travel comes up. People conjure up images of overcoat-clad strangers with aluminum attaché cases handcuffed to their sides, handing them the package that lands an innocent traveler in a Third World prison. If this sound about right, you've been watching too much late-night television.

Air courier companies are established businesses who handle only legitimate freight. They have to vouch for the contents of the mailbags on every flight. If one package contained contraband, the entire time-sensitive shipment could be held indefinitely as evidence. The companies could not afford the loss of reputation that this would cause; a courier company caught smuggling would never get another customer. In order to guarantee to their customers the complete security of the shipment, they usually don't even let you touch the mailbags.

What's more, the bags are usually sealed, so that you could not easily open them even if you were allowed to handle them. As a further precaution, many courier companies routinely x-ray all packages in order to detect contraband. When something suspicious is found, they alert customs at the departure point, and the rest of the shipment is allowed to proceed without delay.

Every customs agent we interviewed agreed that there is virtually no risk of being stopped for possession of contraband while working as a freelance air courier. Not a single agent had heard of a case where a courier was caught unknowingly smuggling contraband. Apparently, the smugglers prefer to use their own people for such purposes.

I spoke with United States Customs Service Public Affairs Officer Mike Fleming in order to get the official word on this issue. True to his role as a law enforcement official, he warned travelers to avoid suspicious situations. "If someone approaches you informally at the airport and asks you to bring a suitcase to his sister," he said, "red warning flags should pop up in your mind."

When you approach a courier company and ask them if you can fly as a courier, you have initiated the interaction. This is very different from the situation above. According to Fleming, the risk of carrying contraband as a freelance courier is "very minimal. I'm not aware of any instances of seizures involving individuals flying as couriers for a legitimate shipping company."

Both customs officials and airline employees are extremely familiar with the courier clearance procedure, which they perform daily. They are in a good position to give an impartial opinion on the matter of courier safety, and across the board they report that courier travel is safe. In fact, you probably have much more to fear from the airline food than you do from the cargo you are accompanying.

HOW TO TRAVEL WITH A COMPANION

Courier companies generally offer only one seat on each flight. That can make it hard to travel with a companion. However, with a little planning, it's fairly easy for two or more travelers to take advantage of these great money-saving flights. One option is to book with a courier broker. Brokers deal with several different courier companies and may have two courier seats on the same flight, on the same day.

Another option is for each of you to fly the same courier route on consecutive days. The first to arrive can handle such details as getting the hotel room and reconnoitering the city, so that everything is ready when the second person arrives. This can be a minor inconvenience, but it is worth the dramatic savings on the airfare.

Of course, if your companion is being stubborn or inflexible, he or she can always pay full coach fare, and book on the same flight on which you will act as a courier. Better yet, get your companion a consolidator ticket for the same flight. It will not be as cheap as your courier fare, but you will both have saved a bundle.

ON THE DAY OF THE FLIGHT...

On your day of departure, you must be at the company's designated meeting point about two hours before the flight. Some companies simply arrange to have you meet their agent right at the airport. Others require their couriers to go to the courier company offices, from which they are escorted by a company employee to the airport.

The agent will stand in line with you at the airport, check you onto the flight, and give you your instructions and the document pouch. The pouch contains the shipping manifests, which are an official listing of the contents of the mailbags you are accompanying. In most cases, you never actually touch any mailbags—for security reasons, the company's staff checks those directly onto the plane.

You board the plane and fly just like any other passenger. (Well, you may be smiling a little more, since you know you paid much less than everyone else did.) When you arrive at your destination, you walk through customs, hand the pouch to the courier representative at the airport, and you're on vacation! The company's local staff handles the mailbags, so you don't even have to wait for your baggage at the carousel. Sometimes you may not even have to meet anyone at the destination airport. Some companies now ask you to call their local office from a pay phone once you have cleared customs.

In some Third World countries, and in a few stubborn industrial nations as well, you may still be required to go to the baggage carousel, recover all of the mailbags, and roll them on a cart through customs. This is rare, but is simple enough and certainly worth the savings.

On the way home, you often have no courier duties. That means you have full use of your checked luggage space, to bring home all those souvenirs. If your flight involves round trip courier duties, you follow the same procedure as you did on the first half of the trip.

DIFFERENT COMPANIES, DIFFERENT POLICIES

There is a great deal of variability in the policies of the twenty or so courier companies listed in this guide. Some companies use only the space of one of your checked bags, while others use your entire checked baggage allotment. Similarly, some companies use your services only on the trip to your destination, while others take up your baggage allowance on your return trip as well. Some give you a huge discount off the regular airfare (up to 85 percent off), while others reduce the fare as little as possible while still filling all of their flights.

Lastly, most companies allow only short, fixed-length stays at your destination, while a few are extremely flexible about your return. The simpler logistics of making all courier assignments one week long are attractive to the courier companies; they automatically know who will be covering each return flight. Nonetheless, longer stays seem to be the wave of the future, as courier companies compete with each other for the limited pool of travelers who know about courier flights.

THE SECRET OF FLYING FREE

Courier companies usually charge you about half of the coach fare for your flight. However, sometimes a courier cancels his reservation at the last-minute. This puts the courier company in a real bind, but it can be a real opportunity for you. When someone cancels more than two days before the flight, the company will try to sell the seat, often at a hefty discount. (Look for companies who offer last-minute discounts in the courier listings, below.)

In the end, someone must accompany those mailbags. The company wants to avoid sending an employee, because it would have to pay for his wages, hotel, and meals while he is abroad.

Instead, the company will cut its losses, and send an independent courier for free! To get in on this deal, you must be willing to fly on less than 48-hours notice. These offers happen frequently. Sometimes you have to be lucky and call them at the right time in order to take advantage of a cancellation that just occurred. Other companies keep an index card file of people who are willing to fly to a particular des-

---

COURIER FLIGHTS

PROS

1   Extremely cheap airfare

2   Less baggage to carry—with carry-ons only, you can skip the whole baggage carousel experience, and get on with your vacation

3   Occasional VIP treatment by airline employees

CONS

1   Usually no checked baggage allowance

2   Often non-refundable, non-changeable tickets

3   Limited choice of schedules and destinations

4   Often restrictions on length of stay (1–4 weeks)

5   Minimum age of 18 years on some flights

tination at the last-minute. These companies will actually call you and ask you if you are interested in filling their suddenly available flight. Because the person who cancelled forfeits his payment, you have the chance to fly cheap, and maybe even free.

If these impromptu flights interest you, call the companies who offer a last-minute phone list (see courier company listings, in the next section) and tell them that you are available. Couriers who have previously flown with that courier company will have priority, since they have proven themselves to be reliable, but first-time couriers may also be accepted. Keep a bag packed—sometimes they call you the same day!

Another option, if you are feeling especially adventurous, is to call around to see if any company has a cancellation that it needs to fill. If you just want to get away, and destination doesn't matter, you can usually find something. And you can't beat the price! Last-minute flights are most common in the low season, or on holiday weekends. From mid-May to September, the system is overloaded with students, making your chances for catching a last-minute flight much slimmer. If you want to fly courier in the summertime, try to book as early as possible.

INDUSTRY INSIDER: EDWARD HASBROUCK

Advice on Which Mode of Travel is Best for Your Needs

A common mistake people traveling abroad make is to project too much of their domestic travel experience onto international travel, which has rules and patterns all its own. There are several very different categories of air travel:

(1) Domestic travel within a single country—published fares are almost always the only option in this case. Sometimes it is much cheaper to buy tickets outside the country, sometimes much cheaper inside the country, and sometimes to buy domestic tickets in conjunction with international tickets, or include domestic stops on a through international ticket. Consulting a good agent about domestic travel before you buy your international ticket can sometimes save you a great deal more than most people imagine.

(2) International round trip excursions (for short stays up to about

three months maximum on most routes)—courier travel and charter flights are usually appropriate for these sorts of trips. The best deals on consolidator tickets on these routes are often found from ethnic specialty agencies, which market to members of immigrant communities who wish to visit their home countries. (London's Sihk-run agencies specializing in India are a good example of this.) Airlines occasionally even offer extremely restricted but otherwise competitive published fares on these routes.

(3) International one-way trips, long-stay trips (which often must be ticketed as two one-way trips), and multi-stop trips (which include around-the-world and circle-Pacific trips)—these are where consolidators are essentially the only cheap choice, and in some cases only the best consolidators will have any deals at all on more unusual routes.

How to Use the
Budget Travel Directory

CHAPTER 2

If you already have a destination in mind, look it up in the index at
the end of the Guide on page 236 to find out what companies will
get you there. The directory is organized by budget travel hub city,
and frequently, the hub city with the most connections to a given destination is also one of the cheapest stepping stones to that destination. So if the flights direct from your nearest hub city fail to meet
your needs, be creative—consider paths through other convenient
hubs as viable (and often superior) alternatives to direct flights.

The hub cities are organized by region: North America, Europe, and
Asia and Australia. Within the regions, each hub city has its own
chapter which lists the companies with the cheapest airfares on
departures from that city.

THE MINIGUIDES

Our **Miniguides** provide a brief introduction to each hub city. The
Market Trends section explains the conditions in the local airfare
market, such as the likelihood of finding discount travel agents there,
and particularly good deals typically available from that hub.

Residents of a particular hub can skip the rest of that city's miniguide.
It is written for travelers unfamiliar with your city, who are using it as
a jumping-off point for further travel. The miniguides provide the
traveler who is **Stopping Over** with enough budget travel information to make for a short, but pleasant stay in each hub. We track
down the city's **Cheap Sleeps** and **Cheap Eats** for you, and point
out details for getting **To and From the Airport**. Finally, we suggest
one **Unique** thing to do in each hub—one interesting (but not
tourist-infested or "typical") activity which will help give you a flavor
of the city.

COMPANY LISTINGS

The company listings themselves provide most of the information you
will need. However, once you have chosen a company, make sure you
get all the details from them. It is your responsibility (and good common sense) to have the latest, most complete information before you

buy your tickets or sign any agreements.

Sample Round Trip Fares are just that—they merely represent the kind of discounts you can expect from each of the companies listed. All sample fares are based on figures quoted by the listed companies for October 1994. These fares will change over time, so it is up to you to call and obtain current fares. Last-minute fares can be even cheaper. The sample fares don't include applicable departure taxes. **Standard Economy Fares** are supplied in order to give the reader a basis for evaluating the sample fares provided by listed companies. The Standard Economy Fares were obtained courtesy of *The Official Airline Guides Electronic Edition Travel Service*. These fares are the cheapest published standard economy fares with minimal or no advance purchase or minimum stay requirements, as available for round trip travel in October 1994.

Please note that the sample fares change constantly. However, they do not vary too much relative to standard economy fares. A fifty percent savings off of standard fares will probably remain unchanged even as the standard fares themselves rise and fall. Because our strategies save you money when fares are high and when fares are low, a good deal today will likely still be a good deal tomorrow.

The **Address** information is provided for your convenience, but we encourage you to contact companies by telephone only. Most companies prefer that you contact them by telephone, and are very slow to respond by mail or fax, if they respond at all. Especially in the case of courier companies, communicating by telephone demonstrates that you understand how the industry works.

Telephone and Fax numbers: we provide them in the format "city code, number" [example: ☎ (071) 555 1212]. If you are calling from outside the country, you should drop any zeros at the start of the city code, and dial the international access code and country code before dialing the number [example: ☎ 011 44 (71) 555 1212]. The country code is listed in the miniguide to each city.

A **Contact** is listed if the company is large and a particular person is responsible for booking flights.

Times to Call: some companies only handle incoming calls at specific times, others have non-traditional office hours. If an informational recording is available, we indicate that here as well.

The **Type of Provider** item tells you whether this company is a discount travel agent, a charter company, or a courier company, and whether they are a full-fledged courier company or a booking agent for such a company.

The **Areas of Specialty** listing helps you focus on companies operating from a certain hub city to the region of your choice. If a company does not specialize, we enter the term "worldwide" here. Sometimes the best fares are found through companies that specialize in a particular geographic region. Use the "areas of specialty" listing to limit your search to a few good choices. Then call them and let them know that you are serious, and will buy if the price is right. Nobody in this business has time to figure out the absolute best deal on a complicated itinerary for someone who is "just looking."

The **Destinations Chart** provides you with the destinations served by each company from the hub city. In the case of charter operators and discount travel agents with too many flights to list, we provide a representative sample of fares for your convenience. If "n/a" appears under Sample Round Trip Fare, this flight had been offered before, but was not available at press time. Call the company to check whether the flight has been resumed. Similarly, a "tba" under Sample Round Trip Fare that the fare is to be announced. For courier companies, we also list the **Length of Stay** for each flight. As mentioned in Chapter 1, courier assignments usually last for a fixed period of time (e.g. two weeks). If there is flexibility in booking your return flight, we indicate the range of possibilities (e.g. 7 to 30 days). If we use commas and/or the word "or," then you have limited flexibility in return dates (e.g. 7, 9 or 14 days).

The area below the Destinations Chart is loaded with useful tidbits of information. For instance, **Annual Fee** refers to the charge that some courier companies impose on you for the privilege of using their services. You may want to avoid these companies unless they still offer the lowest fare, even after you figure in the fee.

A **Deposit** serves as a guarantee to a courier company that you will show up for both halves of your flight. It is often paid by credit card, and refunded upon your return. Do not, under any circumstances, fail to comply with your obligatory courier duties on the return flight. It puts the courier company in the nearly impossible situation of having to find a courier on a few hours notice. Last minute cancellations have two effects: first, you get blacklisted by that company (and probably others) and will likely never again be accepted for a courier flight; second, some companies get fed up with freelance couriers, and stop using them entirely.

Payment Methods are outlined for you—I suggest that you favor companies which allow you to pay by credit card. In the rare event that something goes wrong with your ticket, your credit card company can get you a refund. When possible, use a local company—it is usually easier to resolve any questions or problems that may arise. By all means, please notify me by mail if you ever have any problems with any of the companies listed in this guidebook.

If the listing indicates that you have no **Courier Duties on Return Trip**, you may be able to check luggage or change the dates for your return flight. Remember, most courier flights allow you to bring carry-on luggage only.

Many courier companies require that their couriers be of a certain age. If that is the case, we indicate it under **Minimum Age.**

The **In Business Since** heading tells you when a company was founded. Often this date helps indicate the stability of a given provider.

It is wise to reserve your courier flight as early as possible. To this end, we include a date range called **Recommended Advance Reservations**. The first half of the date range notes how far in advance you should book, so as to get the date you want. Availability is still adequate this far in advance. The second half of the date range denotes the farthest in advance that you could possibly make a reservation. No company will let you reserve a seat more than a year ahead of time, but many open their books about three months before each flight. If you call on the earliest possible day, you are likely to get exactly the flight you want. As always, you can call at the last-minute, too, but you will be looking for cancellations, not picking the date of your choice.

If there are one-way courier flights, last-minute discounts, standby flights, or cancellation phone lists, we'll tell you in the comments section. Other interesting facts and tidbits of information about the company are listed here as well.

A NOTE ABOUT CHANGE

Keep in mind that flights, destinations, and prices are constantly changing. We list prices only reluctantly, because we know that the minor details will change quickly. The fares listed are meant to illustrate the savings you can expect to receive, but the actual prices will have changed. Call the companies to get their current prices. Also agencies do come and go. The agencies we have listed here are well-established, experienced operations that are consistently able to offer better deals than the airlines themselves. That much, we can promise you, will not change.

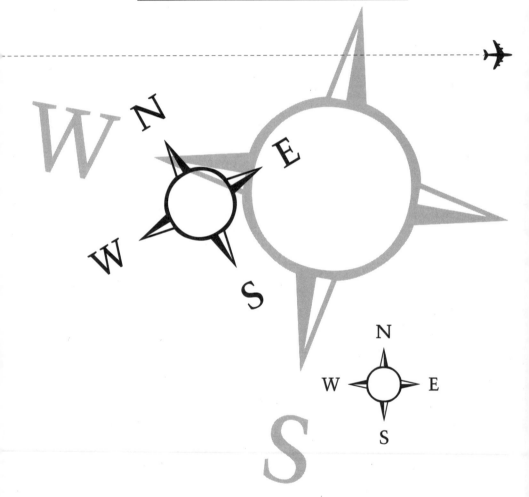

BUDGET TRAVEL BY HUB CITY

CHICAGO, U.S.A.

MARKET TRENDS

By reclaiming Midway airport, carriers like Kiwi, American Trans Air, and Midway Air have made domestic flights from Chicago surprisingly affordable. Courier flights are also available for international flights to **London** and **Mexico City**, although we expect that more destinations will come on line in 1995. Ethnic specialty agencies offer consolidated fares to **Asia** and **Central Europe**. Most foreign tourists need an onward ticket to get into the United States.

STOPPING OVER IN CHICAGO

The **Loop** is the strategic center of Chicago. Business, government and culture congregate here, in the area which was once served by a "loop" of trolley cars. Now it is the "el," or elevated train, which transports commuters from the many suburbs into downtown.

Gusts do swirl off Lake Michigan and through the dense forest of skyscrapers in the Windy City, but the metropolis actually owes its nickname to windbag politicians. One local describes Chicago weather as the worst of both worlds: whiteouts that can shut the whole city down in the winter, and near body-temperature heat with 98 percent humidity in the summer.

Maybe it's due in part to the weather that the blues is such a force in Chicago. The Windy City has arguably the best live music scene in North America. They have even named a street after venerable blues man Muddy Waters. Grab a copy of *Chicago Magazine* for details on the city's innumerable nightspots, including a list of who's playing.

For a taste of that famous Chicago blues, check out the **Kingston Mines** [1007 North Halsted, across the street from Blues Etc. in Lincoln Park, ☎ (312) 477 4646]. Near DePaul University, the **Wise Fools Pub** offers live blues acts in a dive-bar setting, seven days a week [2270 North Lincoln Avenue, ☎ (312) 929 1510].

At night, the mobs descend on **Rush Street**, in the southern part of the Gold Coast. The singles scene is so overwhelming that the Chicago Police close down **Division Street** on some weekends, allowing the crowds to spill over into the streets. Take the el to the

CHAPTER 3

TELEPHONE
COUNTRY CODE:

(1)

CURRENCY:
Dollar
US$1.00 = £0.62

Clark-Division station, because you won't find parking in this area. **Butch McGuire's** [20 West Division Street at North Dearborn, ☎ (312) 337 9080] is the bar that started it all. Butch claims that since it opened in 1961 his bar has made possible the meeting and marriage of over 3,000 couples .

To catch a glimpse of the frenetic activity at **The Chicago Board of Trade** [141 West Jackson Boulevard], just pop into the visitor's center on the Fifth Floor. This is the largest commodities futures exchange in the world—watch as the pork bellies fly, and brokers frantically signal "Buy. Buy! Uh-oh!!!! SELL! SELL! FOR THE SAKE OF GOD, SELL!!!" Watch the drama unfold during free tours, offered on the hour every morning.

For a great view of the Chicago skyline, climb the **John Hancock Center** [875 North Michigan Avenue] instead of the Sears Tower. You won't find tourists blocking your view, and the sunsets from Hancock's 94th floor observation deck are remarkable. Since there is a fee for the observation deck, many folks head up to the 96th floor **Images Lounge**, where they can get a drink and a view for the same price. Or you might rent a bike and explore the 26 miles of waterfront bicycle paths along Lake Michigan. **Lincoln Park** is a great place to start.

CHEAP SLEEPS

Arlington House International Hostel
616 Arlington Place
Chicago, IL 60614 USA
☎ (800) HOSTEL 5, (312) 929 5380
Fax 312/ 665 5485

This mega-hostel has over 200 rooms and can handle upwards of a 1,000 travelers. Located four blocks from the lake in upmarket **Lincoln Park**—where the young, trendy locals hang out—the hostel is walking distance from hundreds of live reggae, rock, and blues venues. The hostel itself has two parties a week, and maintains a friendly atmosphere. There are common lounges, a shared kitchen, and barbecues on Sundays. The hostel shares the building with a retirement home, an arrangement which both sides seem to enjoy. Dorm rooms go for $13 with Rucksacker, AAIH, IYHF or ISIC cards, or

$16 without. Private rooms are $30 single, $34 double, and should be reserved two days in advance.

International Youth Hostel

6318 North Winthrop Avenue
Chicago, IL 60660 USA
☎ (312) 262 1011

Dorm beds go for $13 a night at this clean, friendly120 bed hostel. Private rooms are $35 but they fill up quickly (you can reserve two weeks in advance, by sending a money order for the first night). There are kitchen and laundry facilities, and a communal lounge. Located seven miles north of downtown (near the Loyola University el station), this quiet neighborhood has its own bars and restaurants.

CHEAP EATS

Chicago pizza is thick, oozing with sauce and melted cheese, and delicious. We're talking up to two inches thick, which makes it impossible to eat without a knife and fork. The locals favor the dark, tattered atmosphere of **Gino's East Pizzeria** [160 East Superior Street at North Michigan, ☎ (312) 943 1124]. Go early or late in order to avoid the lines.

When it comes to late night eats, DePaul's **The Wiener Circle** [2622 North Clark Street, ☎ (312) 477 7444] is an institution. The fries, dogs, burgers and obnoxious counter staff are famous.

TO & FROM THE AIRPORT

From any terminal at O'Hare Airport, follow the CTA signs to the el station. For about $1.50 you can catch a 45-minute train to the Loop, where you can also transfer to local buses or other trains. The el runs 24 hours a day, and is the transportation mode of choice among airport employees.

From Midway Airport, you can also take the el to the Loop ($1.50). The last train departs the airport at 11pm, and the trip lasts 30 minutes.

UNIQUELY CHICAGO

To see Chicagoans (at least the North Siders) at their uninhibited best, take in a **Chicago Cubs** baseball game. The ivy-covered walls of Wrigley Field ring one of America's classic ballparks. Bleacher seats are both the cheapest and the most social, but they usually sell out far in advance. Not to worry. Our sources tell us you can always buy tickets from scalpers for as little as face value ($6) depending on the weather and the opponent. Buy a hot dog or a bag of peanuts in order to get the full effect of the experience. Those not horribly familiar with baseball may enjoy the activity in the stands as much as that on the field. Foreign travelers may find asking questions about the game to be an effective way to meet the locals, especially when the Cubs are winning. Take the el to **Wrigley Field** (Addison Street Station), and consider a stop at one of the many nearby bars for pre-game "warm-ups."

Council Travel

1153 North Dearborn Street, Second Floor
Chicago, IL 60610 USA
☎ (800) 743 1823, (312) 951 0585
Fax 312/ 951 7473

Times to Call: 9am to 5pm
Type of Provider: Discount travel agent
Areas of Specialty: Worldwide

DESTINATIONS	SAMPLE ROUND TRIP FARE	STANDARD ECONOMY FARE
Athens	$709	$1,468
Bangkok	$1,069	n/a
London	$590	$878
Milan	$615	$1,018
Tel Aviv	$878	$1,410

Payment Methods: Cash, money order, personal check, Visa,
MasterCard
In Business Since: 1947

The Council on International Educational Exchange (CIEE) is a non-profit organization dedicated to the pursuit of work, study and travel abroad. Council's roots are in student travel, which still makes up the bulk of its business. However, there has been a trend in recent years towards offering more programs for the general public.

Founded in 1947, CIEE initially got students to Europe by sea, using recycled World War II troop ships provided by the U.S. government. From these humble beginnings, it has grown into the largest operator of charter flights from the U.S. to Europe. CIEE has incorporated two travel companies, Council Travel and Council Charter. Council Travel will book you on the cheapest flight they can find for you, whether it's a Council Charter flight (America's oldest charter company), another company's charter flight, or a discounted ticket on a scheduled airline. Some interesting Council Charters run from New York to Rome or Amsterdam.

CIEE is formed by 210 members worldwide, mostly universities. In 1967 CIEE renamed itself in order to encompass added programs for studying or working abroad. If you are interested in such programs, contact Council Travel. They can guide you through the web of gov-

31

ernmental red tape, and make your international experience easier. Council Travel also sells travel gear, rail passes and student IDs.

Cut Rate Travel

1220 Montgomery Drive
Deerfield, IL 60015 USA
☎ (800) 388 0575, (708) 405 0575
Fax 708/ 405 0587

Times to Call: 8am to 7pm, seven days a week
Type of Provider: Consolidator
Areas of Specialty: Worldwide except the USA and Canada

DESTINATIONS	SAMPLE ROUND TRIP FARE	STANDARD ECONOMY FARE
Amsterdam	$479	$828
Buenos Aires	$979	$2,152
Budapest	$679	n/a
Frankfurt	$489	$968
London	$479	$878
Moscow	$679	n/a
Paris	$439	$758
Rio de Janeiro	$989	n/a
Rome	$496	$908
San Jose	$479	$763
Sydney	$1,099	$2,337
Tel Aviv	$850	$1,410

Payment Methods: Cash, personal check, Visa, MasterCard, American Express
In Business Since: 1982

99.9 percent of all agencies do domestic flights—Cut Rate does not, except for connections on international flights. They are true international specialists.

Cut Rate stays open evenings and weekends in order to make things more convenient for travelers. They also have special deals for students, those traveling on short notice, and people who need a one-way flight.

Dependable Travel

3011 South Wolf Road
Westchester, IL 60154 USA
☎ (708) 409 1600
Fax 708/ 409 1612

Times to Call: 9am to 5:30pm
Type of Provider: Courier booking agent
Areas of Specialty: Worldwide

DESTINATIONS	SAMPLE ROUND TRIP FARE	STANDARD ECONOMY FARE	LENGTH OF STAY
London	$459	$878	7 to 60 days
Mexico City	$199	$389	up to 60 days

Payment Methods: Cash, money order, certified check,
personal check
Minimum Age: 18 years
In Business Since: 1984
Recommended Advance Reservations: 6 to 8 weeks

All flights are on Halbart Express courier runs. Look for Halbart to add service to new cities, potentially including some from Chicago, starting in 1995. Dependable will book consolidator fares for companions of those wishing to take a courier flight and still travel with a friend. Call to check on last-minute discounts, which tend to occur in January and February to London, and every few weeks for Mexico. Discounts can be well more than 50 percent off.

This company maintains a cancellation phone list for people who can be at the airport with in five to ten hours notice (Chicago and Milwaukee area residents only).

Japan Budget Travel

104 South Michigan Avenue, Suite 702
Chicago, IL 60603 USA
☎ (800) 843 0273, (312) 236 9797
Fax 312/ 236 8536

Times to Call: 9am to 5pm
Type of Provider: Consolidator
Areas of Specialty: Asia

DESTINATIONS	SAMPLE ROUND TRIP FARE	STANDARD ECONOMY FARE
Bangkok	$1,191	n/a
Hong Kong	$1,011	$2,676
Seoul	$1,080	$1,456
Tokyo	$820	$1,550

Payment Methods: Cash, personal check, Visa, MasterCard, American Express
In Business Since: 1987

Mena Travel

2479 North Clark Street
Chicago, IL 60614 USA
☎ (800) 536 6362, (312) 472 5361
Fax 312/ 472 2829

Times to Call: 9am to 6:30pm
Type of Provider: Consolidator
Areas of Specialty: Latin America

DESTINATIONS	SAMPLE ROUND TRIP FARE	STANDARD ECONOMY FARE
Bogota	$591	$849
Buenos Aires	$952	$2,152
San Salvador	$486	$894
Guatemala City	$408	$837
Lima	$724	n/a
Mexico City	$295	$389
Rio de Janeiro	$1,030	n/a

Payment Methods: Cash, money order, certified check, Visa, MasterCard, American Express
In Business Since: 1965

Mena sells both to travel agents and to the public. They also offer land packages to most of Latin America.

Sunbeam Travels

30 North Michigan Avenue, Suite 1015
Chicago, IL 60602 USA
☎ (800) 433 3161 (Chicago-area only), (312) 263 7664
Fax 312/ 263 0587

Times to Call: 9am to 5:30pm
Type of Provider: Consolidator
Areas of Specialty: Europe, Africa, Middle East, India

DESTINATIONS	SAMPLE ROUND TRIP FARE	STANDARD ECONOMY FARE
Amsterdam	$630	$828
Bombay	$1,200	n/a
Lagos	$1,299	n/a
London	$630	$878
Paris	$640	$758
Tel Aviv	$899	$1,410

Payment Methods: Cash, money order, certified check, personal
check. Will accept credit cards in person only.
In Business Since: 1982

Additional offices in Los Angeles, New York, and Washington, DC.
The majority of their business is sales to travel agents. Have your
dates, departure city and destination ready before you call.

TFI Tours

34 West 32nd Street
New York, NY 10001 USA
☎ (800) 745 8000
Fax 212/ 564 4081

Times to Call: 8:30am to 10pm weekdays, 9am to 8pm Saturday,
10am to 8pm Sunday
Type of Provider: Consolidator
Areas of Specialty: Worldwide

DESTINATIONS	SAMPLE ROUND TRIP FARE	STANDARD ECONOMY FARE
Amsterdam	$410	$828
California	$260	$575
Frankfurt	$620	$968

Chicago			
London	$570		$878
New York	$98		$376
Paris	$580		$758
Rome	$620		$908

Payment Methods: Cash, money order, certified check, Visa, MasterCard, American Express, Discover
In Business Since: 1982

TFI consolidates for 55 different airlines, including most of the major U.S. carriers. They sell to travel agents as well as the public, all via their New York office.

UniTravel Corp.

1177 North Warson Road
St. Louis, MO 63132 USA
☎ (800) 325 2222
Fax 314/ 569 2503

Times to Call: 8:30am to 8:30pm
Type of Provider: Nationwide consolidator
Areas of Specialty: Europe and domestic USA

DESTINATIONS	SAMPLE ROUND TRIP FARE	STANDARD ECONOMY FARE
Atlanta to Amsterdam	$528	$788
Miami to Amsterdam	$550	$1,138
Miami to Paris	$550	$1,696
New York to Paris	$495	$1,360
San Francisco to Frankfurt	$689	$2,294
San Francisco to London	$563	$1,498
San Francisco to Moscow	$823	$2,235

Payment Methods: Cash, money order, certified check, Visa, MasterCard, American Express
In Business Since: 1968

OK, so these guys aren't even in Illinois. Often their fares are low enough to make it worthwhile to do business with them anyway. And while they are listed in the Chicago chapter, they sell tickets for departures from anywhere in the United States. In fact, they also sell discounted tickets with origination points in Europe and Latin

America.

Unitravel is one of the most highly automated providers of discount airfares in the world. They sell primarily to retail travel agents, but they do accept calls from the public. Don't expect a lot of coaching from them—have your dates, destination and departure city ready when you call.

Unitravel consolidates for major airlines like British Airways, Air France, and Delta Airlines. They now offer good fares to South America and South Africa in addition to their European and American destinations. On their best domestic deals, there is a two-day advance purchase clause, but no Saturday night stay is required.

LOS ANGELES, USA

MARKET TRENDS

Los Angeles is home to a robust market for consolidator, charter and courier flights. Consolidator offerings are good for Latin America and Europe, while charters are available to Europe and the Caribbean. Courier deals focus on Australia and Asia, although occasionally London flights are available. Most foreign tourists need an onward ticket to get into the United States. Pick up the Sunday "Travel" section of the *Los Angeles Times* to find advertisements for discount airfares.

STOPPING OVER IN LOS ANGELES

"The City of Angels," while technically the proper translation, is really a misnomer for Los Angeles. The City of Autos might be more accurate. In order to survive for any length of time here, you should consider obtaining a vehicle. The sprawling metropolitan area requires two hours to drive across, and no two attractions are within walking distance of each other.

Culturally, Los Angeles is the land of the "beautiful people." Because of the preponderance of aspiring actors, Los Angeles has some of the best-looking restaurant staffs in the world. Courtesy of the booming plastic-surgery industry, you will see plenty of healthy, wrinkle-free senior citizens cruising about in their convertible BMW's. Even the city's espresso-guzzling slackers are apt to be tan and fit in this image-before-substance enclave.

CHEAP SLEEPS

Santa Monica International Youth Hostel
1436 Second Street
Santa Monica, CA 90401 USA
☎ (310) 393 9913

One of the best hostels in Los Angeles runs only $15 a night. Youth Hostel Association membership is required June through September. It's a beautiful wood-and-brick building one block from the Third Street promenade, a fun place to hang out. 238 beds, reserve in sum-

TELEPHONE COUNTRY CODE:
(1)
CURRENCY:
Dollar
US$1.00 = £0.62

mer. There's a good bulletin board for ride shares and whatnot. The pleasant patio area is a good place to meet other travelers.

Airport Interclub Hostel

2221 Lincoln Boulevard
Venice, CA 90291 USA
☎ (310) 305 0250

A private hostel which allows drinking, socializing, smoking, and mural painting. $15 a night, 74 beds, prefers international visitors, and has a ride board if you're looking to head out of Los Angeles.

Banana Bungalow

2775 Cahuenga Boulevard
West Hollywood, CA 90068 USA
☎ (800) 446 7835, (213) 851 1129
Fax 213/ 851 1569

You'll find amenities galore at this hostel—swimming pool, weight room, basketball court, cheap restaurant, free parking, and so on. Private rooms with two double beds are $45 a night for two people, or $55 a night for three or four people. Dorm rooms, with six beds each, go for $15 a night. Tax, linens and a light breakfast are included, and all rooms include bath. Hollywood Boulevard and Universal Studios are only a 15-minute walk away. Reservations are accepted for private rooms only. Get there early to get a dorm room in July and August.

CHEAP EATS

A tip from the Santa Monica International Hostel led me around the block to **The Gallerie Gourmet**, a budget diner's dream. Sixteen small stands line the halls of this food court, located next to the Cineplex Odeon [1439 Third Street Promenade, Santa Monica]. An astounding variety of cheap ethnic foods is available, ranging from Japanese curry, through Mexican and Thai cuisine, pasta, pizza, French fries and more, all for under $5 a person. There are outdoor tables for sharing.

For good, cheap-ish Caribbean food, try **Versailles** [10319 Venice Blvd. at Motor Avenue in Culver City, ☎ (310) 558 3168]. Open daily

11am-10pm. A cool, young crowd favors the simple Cuban fare here.
Not fancy, but popular.

TO & FROM THE AIRPORT

Didn't we tell you to get a car? We mean it. You simply cannot experience Los Angeles properly without one. For bonus points, consider splurging on a convertible.

From LAX, vehicularly impaired folks staying at the Airport Interclub Hostel or the Banana Bungalow can get a free ride from the airport by calling the hostel. Otherwise, to get to downtown, Hollywood, or Santa Monica catch the free shuttle bus "C" from the LAX Shuttle sign. Shuttle C runs every 10 minutes, 24 hours a day, and the ride to the RTD City Bus Center is 10 minutes. From the Bus Center, catch bus No. 439 to Downtown. To Santa Monica, catch Santa Monica Transit Bus No. 3. For RTD Information, call ☎ (213) 626 4455.

A note about customs: travelers arriving at LAX with nothing to declare can save at least 90 minutes by using the "Express Line."

UNIQUELY LOS ANGELES

Stroll down Ocean Front Walk and experience the impromptu carnival that is Venice. Drop by **Muscle Beach** to see quintessential L.A.— tanned, narcissistic bodybuilders pumping large quantities of iron in an open air, beachfront gymnasium. You'll find cheap-and-greasy food stands, if you dare, as well as an ever-changing lineup of street performers, rollerblading models (who share the Strand with a funky rollerblading rock guitarist), dancers, jugglers, and mimes. And of course, there is the beach itself.

Cheap Tickets, Inc.

8320 Lincoln Boulevard, Room 101
Los Angeles, CA 90045 USA
☎ (800) 377 1000, (310) 645 5054
Fax 310/ 645 8555

Times to Call: 6am to 8pm weekdays, 9am to 3pm Saturdays
Type of Provider: Consolidator
Areas of Specialty: Hawaii, domestic USA, and international

DESTINATIONS	SAMPLE ROUND TRIP FARE	STANDARD ECONOMY FARE
Bangkok	$869	$1,604
Honolulu	$249	$918
London	$639	$1,498
Maui	$309	$1,068
Paris	$779	$950
Sydney	$799	$2,994
Tokyo	$589	$2,038

Payment Methods: Cash, money order, certified check, personal
check, Visa, MasterCard, American Express
In Business Since: 1986

Tickets are non-refundable and non-changeable unless specifically
noted by Cheap Tickets. Additional offices in Hawaii, Miami (opens
late 1994), New York, and San Francisco.

Council Travel

1093 Broxton Avenue, Suite 220
Los Angeles, CA 90024 USA
☎ (800) 743 1823, (310) 208 3551
Fax 310/ 208 4407

Times to Call: 9am to 5pm
Type of Provider: Discount travel agent
Areas of Specialty: Worldwide student, youth, and budget travel

DESTINATIONS	SAMPLE ROUND TRIP FARE	STANDARD ECONOMY FARE
Bali	$989	$1,818
Bangkok	$768	$1,604
London	$568	$1,498

New York	$298	$860	
Sydney	$925	$2,994	
Tel Aviv	$818	$1,852	

In Business Since: 1947

Payment Methods: Cash, money order, personal check, Visa, MasterCard

Open from 10am to 2pm Saturdays, for walk-in clients only.

(See the Council Travel listing in the Chicago chapter for company background.)

Discount Travel International (DTI)

169 West 81st Street
New York, NY 10024 USA
☎ (800) FLY 4 DTI, (212) 362 3636
Fax 212/ 362 3236

Times to Call: 10am to 5:30pm
(Informational recording available after hours.)
Type of Provider: Courier booking agent, consolidator and standby broker
Areas of Specialty: Worldwide

DESTINATIONS	SAMPLE ROUND TRIP FARE	STANDARD ECONOMY FARE	LENGTH OF STAY
Courier flights:			
Bangkok	$500	$1,604	12 to 30 days
Hong Kong	$620	$1,892	12 to 30 days
Melbourne	$525	$3,254	12 to 30 days
Seoul	$450	$1,948	12 to 30 days
Singapore	$550	$2,552	12 to 30 days
Sydney	$600	$2,994	12 to 30 days
Consolidated fares:			
Chicago	$250	$600	
New York	$250	$860	
Paris	$500	$950	

Deposit: $100 for courier flights
Payment Methods: Cash, money order, certified check, Visa, MasterCard

Courier Duties on Return Trip: Yes
Minimum Age: 18 years
In Business Since: 1989
Recommended Advance Reservations: 2 to 3 months for courier flights

DTI offers the only toll-free telephone number in the courier business. All DTI departures are booked through their New York office.

One-way tickets are NOT available for courier flights. Call to check on last-minute discounts on courier runs. DTI maintains a cancellation phone list. Some courier flights are on United Airlines, which permits couriers to check one bag. Ask about flights originating in Miami, New York, or San Francisco. DTI gets new consolidator and space-available destinations all the time, so call them to get the latest details. Space-available is the single cheapest way for flexible travelers to fly within the USA. Currently, most of these flights are on Wings of the World and Tower Air.

Singapore and Hong Kong courier flights include a paid overnight stop in Tokyo.

IBC Pacific (International Bonded Courier)
1595 El Segundo Blvd.
El Segundo, CA 90245 USA
☎ (310) 607 0125
Fax 310/ 607 0126
Contact: Yolanda or Jack

Times to Call: 9am to 4pm, Tuesday through Friday
(Informational recording available after hours.)
Type of Provider: Courier company
Areas of Specialty: Pacific Rim

DESTINATIONS	SAMPLE ROUND TRIP FARE	STANDARD ECONOMY FARE	LENGTH OF STAY
Bangkok	$475	$1,604	2 weeks
Hong Kong	$450	$1,892	2 weeks
Manila	$450	$1,624	2 weeks
Seoul	$375	$1,948	9 or 15 days
Singapore	$350	$2,552	Up to 2 mos.

Sydney	$350	$2,994	15 or 19 days	*Los Angeles*
Taipei	$375	$1,479	9 to 15 days*	
Tokyo	$375	$2,038	9 days	

Deposit: $500!
Payment Methods: Cash, money order, certified check, personal check
Courier Duties on Return Trip: Yes
Minimum Age: 21 years
In Business Since: 1988
Recommended Advance Reservations: 6 weeks to 6 months
Luggage: One piece of carry-on only

Cancellation phone list available. Additional offices are located in Miami and New York. *Taipei flights include a free overnight stay in Seoul.

Jupiter Air

6733 South Sepulveda Boulevard, Suite 170
Los Angeles, CA 90045 USA
☎ (310) 670 5123
Fax 310/ 649 2771

Times to Call: 9am to 5pm
Type of Provider: Courier company
Areas of Specialty: Asia

DESTINATIONS	SAMPLE ROUND TRIP FARE	STANDARD ECONOMY FARE	LENGTH OF STAY
Bangkok	$400	$1,604	Up to 30 days
Hong Kong	$480	$1,892	Up to 30 days
London	tba	$1,498	Up to 30 days
Melbourne	tba	$3,154	Up to 30 days
Seoul	$350	$1,948	7 to 30 days
Singapore	$350	$2,552	Up to 30 days
Sydney	tba	$2,994	Up to 30 days
Taipei	tba	S2,038	Up to 30 days

Annual Fee: $35 for a three-year membership
Deposit: $200
Payment Methods: Cash, money order, certified check,

personal check
Courier Duties on Return Trip: Yes
Minimum Age: 18 years
In Business Since: 1988
Recommended Advance Reservations: ASAP to 3 months

Last-minute flights can be had for 50 percent off. The cancellation phone list produces rare but substantial discounts. Jupiter strongly favors repeat business. Additional offices in Bangkok, Hong Kong, New York, San Francisco, Seoul, Singapore, Sydney, Taipei, Tokyo. . .

Hong Kong is Jupiter Air's hub city. Thus it is sometimes possible to reserve a courier flight from Hong Kong to other Asian cities, such as Bangkok or Tokyo. Keep in mind that you must be back in Hong Kong in time for your return flight.

Midnite Express

930 West Hyde Park Blvd.
Inglewood, CA 90302 USA
☎ (310) 330 7096
Fax 310/ 671 0107
Contact: Ms. Linda Ruth

Times to Call: 9am to 10am only
Type of Provider: Courier company
Areas of Specialty: London

DESTINATIONS	SAMPLE ROUND TRIP FARE	STANDARD ECONOMY FARE	LENGTH OF STAY
London	$350	$1,498	2 wks to 6 mos.

Deposit: $500!
Payment Methods: Cash, money order, certified check, personal check, Visa, MasterCard
Minimum Age: 21
In Business Since: 1988
Recommended Advance Reservations: 1 to 6 months
Luggage: Carry-on only on outbound leg, no restrictions on return

A cancellation phone list is available. Midnite Express sends only one courier per week, on Saturday. To get that coveted seat, you should call at 9am on the first day of the month, two months before you wish to fly (e.g., call May 1st to reserve July 15th). To be eligible, you must live in Southern California; that is, within the triangle created by Santa Barbara, Palm Springs, and San Diego.

New Frontiers

5757 West Century Boulevard
Los Angeles, CA 90045 USA
☎ (800) 677 0720
Fax 310/ 338 0708

Times to Call: 9am to 5pm
Type of Provider: Consolidator and charter operator
Areas of Specialty: Worldwide

DESTINATIONS	SAMPLE ROUND TRIP FARE	STANDARD ECONOMY FARE
Paris	$448	$950
Papeete	$598	$2,376

Payment Methods: Cash, money order, certified check, personal check, Visa, MasterCard, American Express
In Business Since: 1967

Discount tickets on Tower Air, American Trans Air, Continental, KLM, American Airlines, and CORSAIR. Started in 1967 by a French law student who was putting together a trip to Morocco for some friends, the entire trip cost a quarter of the price of a round trip air ticket from Paris to Casablanca. Later, he organized a second trip for 300 people, and Nouvelles Frontières (as the company is known in Europe) was born. They now have 132 offices worldwide, and some of the cheapest flights to or from the French-speaking world. Pioneer discounter New Frontiers fought the airline cartel in a landmark 1985 European Court of Justice case, which set the precedent making the sale of cheap tickets in Europe possible.

S.O.S. International Couriers

8715 La Tijera Blvd.
Los Angeles, CA 90045 USA
☎ (310) 649 6640
Fax 310/ 649 1214

Los Angeles

Contact: Margie
Times to Call: 8am to 6pm
Type of Provider: Courier company
Areas of Specialty: Latin America

DESTINATIONS	SAMPLE ROUND TRIP FARE	STANDARD ECONOMY FARE	LENGTH OF STAY
Mexico City	$200	$370	Up to 30 days

Payment Methods: Cash, money order, certified check, personal check
Courier Duties on Return Trip: yes
Minimum Age: 18 years
In Business Since: 1987
Recommended Advance Reservations: 2 to 3 months

Last-minute discounts crop up from time to time. Cancellation phone list for the extremely flexible.

The also offer flights to Mexico City from New York and Miami. Another possibility is a round trip flight to these U.S. hubs from Mexico City. Book all these flights through the Los Angeles office.

STA Travel

920 Westwood Boulevard
Westwood, CA 90024 USA
☎ (800) 777 0112, (310) 824 1574
Fax 310/ 824 2928

Times to Call: 9am to 5pm
Areas of Specialty: Worldwide
Type of Provider: Discount travel agency

DESTINATIONS	SAMPLE ROUND TRIP FARE	STANDARD ECONOMY FARE
Amsterdam	$630	$1,478
Bangkok	$825	$1,604
Frankfurt	$735	$2,295
Hong Kong	$730	$1,892
London	$625	$1,498
Singapore	$845	$2,552
Sydney	$975	$2,994
Tokyo	$615	$2,038

Payment Methods: Cash, money order, certified check, personal check, Visa, MasterCard, American Express
In Business Since: 1975

STA is the world's largest travel organization for students and young, independent travelers. They have 120 locations worldwide. Some of their best fares require student ID, or carry a maximum age.

Their tickets are highly flexible, usually good for one year and requiring no advance purchase. Date changes can be made at any office worldwide for $25; refunds cost only $50 to $75. Such flexible tickets are a wise choice for travelers going on long trips without fully concrete itineraries. STA tickets are priced based on one-way tickets, which makes it easy to book open-jaw flights.

SunTrips

The SunTrips Building
2350 Paragon Drive
San Jose, CA 95131 USA
☎ (800) 786 8747, (408) 432 1101

Times to Call: 7:30am to 6:30pm weekdays, Saturday 9am to 4pm
Type of Provider: Charter operator
Areas of Specialty: Europe, Mexico and domestic USA

DESTINATIONS	SAMPLE ROUND TRIP FARE	STANDARD ECONOMY FARE
Boston	$218	$734
Cancun	$229	$603
Kauai	$289	$1,068
Honolulu	$219	$918
Maui	$239	$1,068
Puerto Vallarta	$149	$516

Payment Methods: Cash, money order, certified check, personal check, Visa, MasterCard, American Express
In Business Since: 1976

SunTrips' coast-to-coast and London flights operate in spring and summer only, except for the Los Angeles to Boston run.

Hawaii and coast-to-coast flights are scheduled service. Mexico and

London are charter flights. London flights use Stansted Airport, which has a direct rail link to the London Underground's Liverpool Station. Most aircraft are provided and operated by Leisure Air, a major charter company. Book Los Angeles flights with your local travel agent, or call their central office in San Jose.

TFI Tours

34 West 32nd Street
New York, NY 10001 USA
☎ (800) 745 8000, (213) 687 3500
Fax 212/ 564 4081

Times to Call: 8:30am to 10pm weekdays, 9am to 8pm Saturday, 10am to 8pm Sunday,
Type of Provider: Consolidator
Areas of Specialty: Worldwide

DESTINATIONS	SAMPLE ROUND TRIP FARE	STANDARD ECONOMY FARE
Bangkok	$800	$1,604
Frankfurt	$700	$2,294
London	$580	$1,498
New York	$318	$860
Paris	$710	$950
Rio de Janeiro	$620	$2,086
Tokyo	$590	$2,038

Payment Methods: Cash, money order, certified check, Visa, MasterCard, American Express, Discover
In Business Since: 1982

TFI consolidates for 55 different airlines, including most of the major U.S. carriers. They sell to travel agents as well as the public. They do have a local telephone number in Los Angeles, but faxes must be sent to the New York office.

Way to Go Travel

6679 Sunset Blvd.
Los Angeles, CA 90028 USA
☎ (213) 466 1126

Times to Call: 9am to 5pm weekdays, 10am to 2pm Saturday
Type of Provider: Courier booking agent and discount travel agency
Areas of Specialty: Europe, Asia, East Coast of USA

DESTINATIONS	SAMPLE ROUND TRIP FARE	STANDARD ECONOMY FARE	LENGTH OF STAY
Courier flights:			
Bangkok	$675	$1,604	Up to 55 days
Djakarta	$700	$1,745	Up to 55 days
Singapore	$600	$2,552	Up to 55 days

DESTINATIONS	SAMPLE ROUND TRIP FARE	STANDARD ECONOMY FARE
Discount flights:		
Amsterdam	$470	$1,478
Chicago	$250	$600
Honolulu	$482	$918
Kingston	$313	$796
New York	$250	$860
Paris	$400	$950

Deposit: $100 to $200
Payment Methods: Cash, money order, certified check,
personal check
Courier Duties on Return Trip: Yes
Minimum Age: 18
In Business Since: 1988
Recommended Advance Reservations: 1 to 3 months for couriers,
anytime for charters
One-way Tickets Available: Very rarely for courier flights
Flexibility of Return Dates: Up to 55 day, fixed

Last-minute discounts are sometimes available. Affiliated offices operate in New York and San Francisco. Prices increase slightly in summertime.

Some of their charter flights are booked on a "space-available" basis, which is why they are so cheap. There is some risk that you would not get on the plane on the date you specified, although the agency claims that a very high percentage of their standby passengers board their first-choice flight. If you don't make it, you try again the next day.

MIAMI

MARKET TRENDS

Miami is the connecting point between Latin American and North American business. This makes for a fabulous variety of courier flights from Miami south. How about flying from Miami to Caracas, Venezuela round trip for $100?! Miami also benefits from an increasingly competitive domestic air travel market all along the East coast, which makes $99 flights to New York possible. Peak season in Miami itself runs from Christmas through the college spring breaks in late March. Prices and hostel occupancy are at their height at this time. Most foreign tourists need an onward ticket to get into the United States.

STOPPING OVER IN MIAMI

Miami's **South Beach** (those in the know call it "SoBe") is quickly gaining a reputation as the American Riviera. Photogenic Art Deco buildings and palm-lined beaches provide quite a backdrop for galleries, restaurants, and visitors from all over the world. Most of the district is listed in the National Register of Historic Places.

The South Beach area was the place to be in the twenties and thirties, when wealthy Cubans and sun-hungry northerners made their annual migrations to see and be seen. The area lost its popularity in subsequent decades, and the famous Art Deco buildings began to deteriorate. The plus side to this fall from grace was the birth of a budget-lodgings sector with unsurpassed scenery. The palm trees, the beaches and the pastel-stuccoed hotels were still there, and the backpacker set could afford to enjoy them. Sadly, this may change by the end of the decade.

The problem, it seems, is the cyclical nature of history. South Beach is hot again. The upscale crowd is moving back. High-fashion models, photographers, and movie stars share the clubs with shoestring travelers, creating quite an international meeting place. And you are never more than a few blocks from the beach. The prices have yet to soar, but they will. Try to check out South Beach before it leaves budget travelers behind. There is more to Miami than South Beach, but you can explore that next time.

TELEPHONE
COUNTRY CODE:

(1)

CURRENCY:
Dollar
US$1.00 = £0.62

One thing Miami Beach is not is a quiet resort town. Nor does it resemble any other city in Florida. There is hedonism at its finest, 24 hours a day, seven days a week. The nightlife starts at midnight, and the after-hours clubs don't open until 5am. Pick up a copy of *New Times* or *Postmortem* to get the scoop on the local club scene, which is constantly changing. Many of the newer chic clubs are centered around Fifth or Sixth Streets and Washington. As a rule, things are less expensive and less touristy a block or so off of Ocean Drive. **The News Café** at Eighth Street and Ocean is where people stop at dawn for a bite to eat on their way home. In fact, this outdoor café is a hub for socializing all day long.

During the daytime, the action is centered on the beach, where people-watching is always in style. The area between Eighth and Twelfth Streets is a good place to meet the locals. To get a feel for the layout of SoBe, walk confidently through the lobby of the **Park Central Hotel**, and catch the elevator up to the rooftop sun deck. The view of the Miami skyline and beaches is fabulous, and the Deco design of the restored hotel is easy on the eyes as well.

CHEAP SLEEPS

The Art Deco district is home to a multitude of hostels and budget hotel options.

Clay Hotel / Hostelling International Miami Beach

1438 Washington Avenue at Espanola Way
Miami Beach, FL 33139 USA
☎ (800) 379 CLAY, (305) 534 2988

Facilities include laundry, kitchen, and a ride board. Private double rooms for $30, include air conditioning for $1 more. Beds in a quad go for $12, for members $9. No curfew, $5 key Deposit.

Tropics

1550 Collins
Miami Beach, FL 33139 USA
☎ (305) 531 0361
Fax 305/ 531 8676

Tacky fliers proclaim a "clublike atmosphere," but it has a freshwater swimming pool ("with Poolbar") and our Miami researcher swears by it. Private rooms for $30 or hostel beds for $12. No curfew.

Miami Beach International Travelers Hostel

236 Ninth Street at Washington Avenue

Miami Beach, FL 33139 USA

☎ (305) 534 0268

Mellow, fun place with a very international clientele. Features laundry, kitchen, the all-important common room with TV and a library, and an outdoor terrace. No curfew. Private rooms for $30 for one or two people, or $12 for a bed in a quad.

CHEAP EATS

For really cheap food, check out the bakeries, fruit stands, and **SB Pita** at 1448A Washington Avenue. **Our Place Natural Foods Eatery**, right across the street from the Miami Beach International Travelers Hostel [830 Washington Avenue, ☎ (305) 674 1322], is a highly recommended vegetarian option. Tasty tofu dishes, salads, soups and more run $3 to $10 a person.

At 7th and Collins, **Puerto Saugua** [☎ (305) 673 1115] offers good Cuban food in a family run restaurant. Don't leave Miami without trying out the subtly spiced Cuban cuisine.

Feel the need to multi-task? While eating at this Thai outdoor café and restaurant, you can also be shopping at its in-house crafts shop. **World Resources** is the name of the place, and it is located at 719 Lincoln Road [☎ (305) 534 5979]. Entrees average about $8.

When you're feeling a bit upscale, try the **Toy Gallery** at 448 Espanola Way [☎ (305) 538 3230] for healthy international cuisine involving lots of fresh seafood and vegetables. Nothing is sautéed, everything is either steamed or roasted. The atmosphere is like a plush backyard, with lots of greenery and patio tables. Live alternative music on weekend nights. Fabulous fresh bread from a local bakery. Shares a courtyard with the Clay Hotel. Entrees run $6 to $12.

TO & FROM THE AIRPORT

Miami International Airport boasts facilities which make other airports look downright unfriendly. Stuck at the airport for a few hours? Work out those built-up aggressions at the little-known **Airport Health Club**, on the eighth floor of the airport's hotel, in Concourse E. Open 6am to 10pm daily. Use of their jogging path, weight room, swimming pool and Jacuzzi will set you back a mere $5. Afterwards, check out the Miami skyline from the Top of the Port Lounge, on the same floor. Weekdays from 5pm to 7pm, they have free hors d'oeuvres, and $1 beers if you ask for the Happy Hour Special. Sometimes they even have live music in the early evening.

For those of you who decide to leave this incredible airport in spite of all it has to offer, the "J" (East) Metro bus runs every 20-30 minutes to Miami Beach. Transfer to the "C" or "K" (South). Fare is $1. To catch the bus from any concourse, proceed downstairs and across the street to the bus loop. SuperShuttle also offers service to South Beach for $13; call (305) 871 2000 or walk out the door near baggage claim and look for their yellow t-shirted representatives. Parking in South Beach is a nightmare, so cars are not advised.

UNIQUELY MIAMI

Buy mosquito repellent, rent a car (don't pay more than $30 a day; check at your hostel for discounts and car sharing ideas) and drive 30 minutes along Route 41 to **Shark Valley**, part of the Everglades National Park. Shark Valley is by no means tourist free, but it is absolutely worth visiting. You can rent a bicycle for $2 an hour, and ride through the exotic, wildlife-filled, 22-mile loop. This is one of the best (and certainly the cheapest) ways to get a taste of the Everglades. Couch potatoes, there is also a tram tour available. And for the highly adventurous, contact the **Visitors' Center [☎ (305) 247 6211]** for advice, trail maps, and canoe or hiking tours. Remember: don't feed the alligators.

A-1 International Courier

PO Box 527850
Miami, FL 33152 USA
☎ (305) 594 1184
Fax 305/ 594 2967
Contact: Nellie

Times to Call: 9am to 5pm
Type of Provider: Courier company
Areas of Specialty: South America

DESTINATIONS	SAMPLE ROUND TRIP FARE	STANDARD ECONOMY FARE	LENGTH OF STAY
Caracas	$150	$198	up to 6 weeks

Payment Methods: Cash, money order, certified check,
personal check.
Courier Duties on Return Trip: Yes
Minimum Age: 18 years
In Business Since: 1989
Recommended Advance Reservations: 2 months

This company maintains a cancellation phone list for Miami area
residents.

Council Travel

One Datran Center, Suite 320
9100 South Dadeland Boulevard
Miami, FL 33156 USA
☎ (800) 743 1823, (305) 670 9261
Fax 305/ 670 9266

Times to Call: 9am to 5pm
Type of Provider: Discount travel agent
Areas of Specialty: Worldwide

DESTINATIONS	SAMPLE ROUND TRIP FARE	STANDARD ECONOMY FARE
Athens	$770	n/a
London	$458	$1,438
Rio de Janeiro	$938	$1,632
San Jose	$298	$656
Tel Aviv	$838	$1,674

In Business Since: 1947

Payment Methods: Cash, money order, personal check, Visa, MasterCard

(See the Council Travel listing in the Chicago chapter for company background.)

Discount Travel International (DTI)

169 West 81st Street
New York, NY 10024 USA
☎ (800) FLY 4 DTI, (212) 362 3636
Fax 212/ 362 3236

Times to Call: 10am to 5:30pm
(Informational recording available after hours.)
Type of Provider: Courier booking agent, consolidator and standby broker
Areas of Specialty: Worldwide

DESTINATIONS	SAMPLE ROUND TRIP FARE	STANDARD ECONOMY FARE
London	$558	$1,438
Mexico City	$198	$566
New York	$150	$598
Rio de Janeiro	$625	$1,632
Sao Paulo	$625	$1,632

Deposit: $100 for courier flights
Payment Methods: Cash, money order, certified check, Visa, MasterCard
Courier Duties on Return Trip: Yes
Minimum Age: 18 years
In Business Since: 1989
Recommended Advance Reservations: 2 to 3 months for courier flights

We commend DTI for offering the only toll-free telephone number in the courier business. All DTI departures are booked through their New York office.

One-way tickets are NOT available for courier flights. Call to check on last-minute discounts on courier runs. DTI maintains a cancellation phone list. Some courier flights are on United Airlines, which permits couriers to check one bag. Ask about flights originating in Los Angeles, New York, or San Francisco. DTI gets new consolidator and space-available destinations all the time, so call them to get the latest details. Space-available is the single cheapest way for flexible travelers to fly within the USA. Currently, most of these domestic flights are on Wings of the World and Tower Air.

Going Places Travel

25 SE Second Avenue, Suite 450
Miami, FL 33141 USA
☎ (305) 373 5813
Fax 305/ 871 9491
Contact: Laura

Times to Call: 9:30am to 6pm
Type of Provider: Courier booking agent
Areas of Specialty: Worldwide

DESTINATIONS	SAMPLE ROUND TRIP FARE	STANDARD ECONOMY FARE	LENGTH OF STAY
Buenos Aires	$400	$1,500	up to 30 days
Caracas	$129	$198	1 week
Guatemala	$200	$672	1 year, open
London	$380	$1,438	1 week
Madrid	$350	$1,170	1 week
Mexico City	$150	$566	varies
Quito	$250	$832	up to 1 month
Rio de Janeiro	$400	$1,632	1 week
Santiago	$400	$1,500	up to 1 month

Payment Methods: Cash, money order, certified check, personal check
Courier Duties on Return Trip: Yes
Minimum Age: 18 years
In Business Since: 1992
Recommended Advance Reservations: 2 months

One-way tickets are available. Call to check on last-minute discounts.

Halbart Express

731 NW 35th Street
Miami, FL 33122 USA
☎ (305) 593 0260
Fax 305/ 593 0158
Contact: Ileana

Times to Call: 10am to 3pm
(Informational recording available after hours.)
Type of Provider: Courier company
Areas of Specialty: Worldwide

DESTINATIONS	SAMPLE ROUND TRIP FARE	STANDARD ECONOMY FARE	LENGTH OF STAY
Madrid	$350	$1,170	1 week
Mexico City	$300	$566	3 to 60 days
Rio de Janeiro	$378	$1,632	9 to 12 days

Deposit: $100
Payment Methods: Cash, money order, certified check,
personal check, Visa, MasterCard
Courier Duties on Return Trip: Yes
Minimum Age: 18 years
In Business Since: 1980
Recommended Advance Reservations: 1 to 3 months

Call to check on last-minute discounts. This company maintains a cancellation phone list. Fares increase by about $100 near Thanksgiving, Christmas, and July to August.

Halbart offers courier flights departing from New York and Miami only. However, offices in Atlanta, Boston, Chicago, Detroit, Los Angeles, and Paris, just may begin booking courier flights in 1995 or 1996.

International Bonded Couriers (IBC)

8401 NW 17th Street
Miami, FL 33126 USA
☎ (305) 591 8080
Fax 305/ 591 2056
Contact: Nora

Times to Call: 10:30am to 6pm

Areas of Specialty: Worldwide

Type of Provider: Courier company

DESTINATIONS	SAMPLE ROUND TRIP FARE	STANDARD ECONOMY FARE	LENGTH OF STAY
Nassau	tba	$160	1 week
Santo Domingo	tba	$330	1 week
Guatemala	tba	$672	1 week
Kingston	tba	$338	1 week
Rio de Janeiro	tba	$1,632	1 week
Santiago	tba	$1,500	1 week

Deposit: $500!

Payment Methods: Cash, money order, certified check, personal check

Courier Duties on Return Trip: Yes

Minimum Age: 21 years

In Business Since: 1984

Recommended Advance Reservations: 2 months for Latin America, 2 weeks for the Caribbean

Luggage: One piece of carry-on only

Additional offices in Los Angeles and San Francisco. IBC keeps a cancellation phone list for you last-minute types.

Interworld Travel

800 Douglas Road, Suite 140

Coral Gables, FL 33134 USA

☎ (800) 468 3793, (305) 443 4929

Fax 305/ 443 0351

Times to Call: 9am to 6pm

Type of Provider: Consolidator

Areas of Specialty: Europe and Africa

DESTINATIONS	SAMPLE ROUND TRIP FARE	STANDARD ECONOMY FARE
Amsterdam	$570	$1,138
Athens	$695	n/a
Frankfurt	$595	$2,992

Johannesburg	$1,395	$2,724
London	$440	$1,438
Nairobi	$1,295	n/a
Paris	$570	$1,696

Payment Methods: Cash, personal check, American Express
In Business Since: 1984

Good source of cheap airfares for the entire southeastern United States, and some flights from anywhere in the United States. The Johannesburg flight is particularly popular because it is direct. The brothers who own Interworld learned the business by working for years in several London bucketshops.

Line Haul Services

7859 NW 15th Street
Miami, FL 33126 USA
☎ (305) 477 0651
Fax 305/ 477 0659

Times to Call: 9am to 5pm
Type of Provider: Courier company
Areas of Specialty: Worldwide

DESTINATIONS	SAMPLE ROUND TRIP FARE	STANDARD ECONOMY FARE	LENGTH OF STAY
Bogota	$200	$790	7 to 21 days
Buenos Aires	$350	$1,500	7 to 21 days
Caracas	$200	$198	7 to 21 days
Guatemala	$200	$672	7 to 21 days
Guayaquil	$200	$832	7 to 21 days
La Paz	$350	$850	7 to 21 days
Lima	$250	$1,348	7 to 21 days
Montevideo	$400	n/a	7 to 21 days
Quito	$200	$832	7 to 21 days
Rio de Janeiro	$400	$1,632	7 to 21 days
Santiago	$400	$1,500	7 to 21 days
Sao Paulo	$400	$1,632	7 to 21 days

Payment Methods: Cash, money order, certified check, personal check

Courier Duties on Return Trip: Yes
Minimum Age: 18 years
In Business Since: 1989
Recommended Advance Reservations: 2 months

Call to check on last-minute discounts.

Martillo Express

1520 West 41st Street
Hialeah, FL 33012 USA
☎ (305) 822 0880
Fax 305/ 558 5890
Contact: Ana Louisa

Times to Call: 9am to 5pm
Type of Provider: Courier company
Areas of Specialty: Worldwide

DESTINATIONS	SAMPLE ROUND TRIP FARE	STANDARD ECONOMY FARE	LENGTH OF STAY
Guayaquil	$200	$832	3 to 60 days
Quito	$200	$832	3 to 60 days

Payment Methods: Cash, money order, certified check
Courier Duties on Return Trip: Yes
Minimum Age: 18 years
In Business Since: 1989
Recommended Advance Reservations: 2 months

Call to check on last-minute discounts. This company maintains a cancellation phone list.

TFI Tours

34 West 32nd Street
New York, NY 10001 USA
☎ (800) 745 8000, (305) 895 8115
Fax 212/ 564 4081

Times to Call: 8:30am to 10pm weekdays, 9am to 8pm Saturday,
10am to 8pm Sunday
Type of Provider: Consolidator
Areas of Specialty: Worldwide

DESTINATIONS	SAMPLE ROUND TRIP FARE	STANDARD ECONOMY FARE
Buenos Aires	$580	$1,500
Caracas	$232	$198
Frankfurt	$600	$2,992
London	$530	$1,438
New York	$158	$598
Paris	$570	$1,696
Rio de Janeiro	$704	$1,632
Rome	$610	$1,368

Payment Methods: Cash, money order, certified check, Visa,
MasterCard, American Express, Discover
In Business Since: 1982

TFI consolidates for 55 different airlines, including most of the major
U.S. carriers. They sell to travel agents as well as the public. From
Miami, they also offer a special "Businessman's Fare" to Caracas. If
you fly down in the morning, and return in the evening, the fare is
only $60 each way.

Trans Air Systems

7264 NW 25th Street
Miami, FL 33122 USA
☎ (305) 592 1771
Fax 305/ 592 2927
Contact: Marisol or Elizabeth

Times to Call: 9am to 5pm
Type of Provider: Courier company
Areas of Specialty: Worldwide

DESTINATIONS	SAMPLE ROUND TRIP FARE	STANDARD ECONOMY FARE	LENGTH OF STAY
Buenos Aires	$350	$1,500	up to 30 days
Guatemala City	$200	$672	up to 30 days
Mendoza	$350	n/a	up to 30 days
Quito	$350	$832	up to 30 days
Santiago	$350	$1,500	up to 30 days

Payment Methods: Cash, money order, certified check,
personal check
Courier Duties on Return Trip: Yes
Minimum Age: 18 years
In Business Since: 1989
Recommended Advance Reservations: 2 months

Call to check on last-minute discounts. This company maintains a
cancellation phone list.

NEW YORK, USA

MARKET TRENDS

Tremendous air traffic volume along with hordes of consolidators and courier companies, make New York a great place to catch a budget flight. The best deals are on flights to Europe. Many of the domestic low-fare airlines serve New York, so it can be a good base from which to see the United States. However, real estate is pricy in the Big Apple, so expect higher-than-average prices for accommodations and food. Most foreign tourists need an onward ticket to get into the United States.

STOPPING OVER IN NEW YORK

New York is a fast-moving, exhilarating, at times overwhelming city. There is so much to do here, it is hard to know where to start. Clearly "dinner and a movie" is out—you can do that back at home. You might catch a Broadway play, if you can find tickets. If not, there's always off-Broadway, and even off-off-Broadway, where you sit close enough to touch the costumes of the talented performers. Maybe the free summer concerts by the Julliard School (see below) are more your style, or the latest exhibit at SoHo's Alternative Museum, or the roller-rink disco near the Central Park Bandshell. The point is, you've got options. Pick up a copy of the *Village Voice* for the week's calendar of events.

By New York, we are really referring to Manhattan. The other boroughs each have a charm of their own. Nonetheless, for a brief visit, Manhattan is the place to be. Huge concrete structures bob like big apples in a frenzy of maniacal cabbies, well-tailored stockbrokers, gaunt-faced poets and fast-moving watch salesmen.

A recent study ranked New York as the second most hostile city in the United States. Far from protesting their newly earned label, New Yorkers were furious that they finished second to Philadelphia! That's not to say that you shouldn't visit New York, but there are a few things you should be aware of. New Yorkers walk fast, talk fast, and boy, you better not get in their way on an escalator. You have to be streetwise to survive here. New Yorkers may have a reputation for being rude, but they've really just learned to keep their guards up all

CHAPTER 6

TELEPHONE
COUNTRY CODE:

(1)

CURRENCY:
Dollar
US$1.00 = £0.62

the time. Do the same, and you will do fine.

Yet while New York can be rough, it can also be romantic. Summer evenings are a great time to go out in New York. During July and August, musicians from the **Juilliard School** give free concerts in the sculpture garden at the **Museum of Modern Art** [14 West 54th Street near 5th Avenue, ☎ (212) 708 9491]. Doors open at 6pm, and the show starts at 8:30pm, Friday and Saturday only. Any time of year, you can catch the surprisingly romantic **Staten Island Ferry**. If you time it right, you get to see the sunset on the way out, and watch the lights come on in Manhattan on your way back. Bring a bottle of wine, and enjoy [take the #1 subway to South Ferry]. If you'd rather take a romantic stroll, walk across the **Brooklyn Bridge** at sunset [Catch the Lexington Line subway (4, 5, or 6) to City Hall].

Unlike most cities in the world, neighborhoods in New York change by the block. One minute you are walking in a decent neighborhood, and a moment later you find yourself in trouble. If this happens to you, just backtrack into a safer area. While it is difficult to judge the safety level of a place by its neighborhood, it is good to be able to orient yourself. The general layout goes like this: Midtown stretches from 23rd Street to 59th Street. Downtown is 23rd Street and below, Uptown is 59th Street and above. The East and West distinction tells you an address' location relative to Fifth Avenue and Central Park.

CHEAP SLEEPS

New York International Hostel (HI)
891 Amsterdam Avenue
New York, NY 10025
☎ (212) 932 2300

This is the largest hostel in the United States, with almost 500 beds. Located in a freshly remodeled landmark building, the hostel has kitchens and dining rooms, common lounges, and an outdoor garden. Open 24 hours, with no curfew. Beds are $20, plus $3 for nonmembers, $3 for sheets, and $2 for towels. Subway: 102nd Street. This Upper West Side spot books up fast, mainly with European travelers.

International House   *New York*

Admissions Office
500 Riverside Drive
New York, NY 10027 USA
☎ (212) 316 8436
Fax 212/ 316 1827

The International House is a graduate dormitory run by a private foundation. It's on the Upper West Side, right next door to Columbia University with easy access to subways. Students, interns, visiting researchers and scholars are its target market, but student and even non-student travelers can take advantage of lower occupancy at International House in the spring, summer, and sometimes even Christmas holidays. The arrangements are Spartan but very secure. One added benefit is the Programs Office, which supplies not only tourist information but insider tips and sometimes freebie event tickets. Regular year residents are another source to find out about the "real" New York. Pay in cash or travelers' checks, or with Visa or MasterCard for bills of $50 or more. The current rate schedule is: 1 to 14 days at $25/day, 15 to 30 days at $18/day, 1 month at $14-18/day (depending on the room). Deluxe rooms are available at $60-90/ night, with air conditioning, cable television and private bathroom; these include large double beds and can accommodate four adults or even a small family.

Banana Bungalow

250 West 77th Street at Broadway
New York, NY 10024 USA
☎ (800) 6 HOSTEL, (212) 769 2441
Fax 212/ 877 5733

The same folks that brought you Los Angeles's most festive hostel have set up shop in the Big Apple. Once construction winds down, look for more of the same friendly, social atmosphere and quality facilities here on the east side of Midtown. Complete renovations are in process, and the place should be fully restored by summer of 1995. Features include a roof-top sun deck, common lounges, and kitchen facilities. Rates are $15-19 a night. For guaranteed reservations, fax ahead your credit card information, along with your name and arrival date.

Another way to avoid the pricy hotels and meet some New Yorkers at the same time is to book with **City Lights Bed and Breakfast**. Hosts tend to be normal New Yorkers who have an extra room or two. Many of them are in the arts, and can give you the scoop on the hottest happenings. Doubles start at $75 a night; unhosted apartments are also available. Call ☎ (212) 737 7049, or write to PO Box 20355, Cherokee Station, New York, NY 10028.

CHEAP EATS

You name the cuisine, they've got it in New York. Yet when push comes to shove, pizza and bagels define the budget food scene.

For bagels, there's no place like family run **Ess-A-Bagels** (359 First Avenue at 21st Street). This place still makes each bagel by hand, and boils them instead of steaming. The result is a proper bagel that's chewy on the inside, and crispy on the outside. Our reviewer said simply, "Amazing!" before falling into a blissful, self-indulgent trance. They have a second store on the east side of Midtown, at 831 3rd Avenue and 50th Street.

Of all the pizzerias in Manhattan, which one is the real "Original Ray's?" The legal battles over the Ray's name rage on, and we don't want to touch them. Nonetheless, our anonymous sources point to **Famous Ray's**, at 465 Sixth Avenue and 11th Street, in the West Village [☎ (212) 243 2253]. You can order by the slice for $2.50. This Ray's uses only natural ingredients to produce a thick, cheesy pizza with a zesty sauce. Legend has it that two pizza-starved Americans studying in London found themselves compelled to fly to New York for a fix of Famous Ray's. They brought 40 pies back to London, and sold them at a profit to pay for their airfares!

For a real "come-as-you-are" kind of place in the East Village, check out **Dojo Restaurant** [24 St. Marks Place, between Second and Third, ☎ (212) 674 9821]. Don't let the tofu and stir-fry fool you, this place also cooks up a mean burger. Full dinners start at $2.95, and the most expensive meal on the menu is $8. They offer good music and outdoor tables to boot.

From JFK, take the free Long Term Parking shuttle from any terminal to the Far Rockaway subway line (A train). The subway takes you to Manhattan in about an hour, for about a buck.

From LaGuardia, catch the Q-33 bus to the end of the line (Roosevelt Avenue), where you can catch the subway into Manhattan. Each leg takes about 20 minutes, and costs $1.25.

From Newark, take New Jersey Transit bus No. 62 to Newark Penn Station (twice hourly from Terminals A, B, and C; $1; 15-minute ride) .Then catch the PATH train to the World Trade Center in Manhattan (again $1, 15-minute ride).

UNIQUELY NEW YORK

In the summertime, you'll find New Yorkers at **Shakespeare in the Park**. The New York Shakespeare Festival sponsors this free event at the open-air **Delacorte Theater** in Central Park. Call (212) 861 7277 for free tickets.

Tickets to tapings of **The Late Show with David Letterman** are much tougher to get, but where else can you get a better feel for New York's collective state of mind? Confirmed tickets must be requested by mail months in advance, but standby tickets are given out at noon each day, at the box office of the Ed Sullivan Theater, 1697 Broadway between 53rd and 54th. Tapings start at 5:30pm.

Air Facility

153-40 Rockaway Boulevard
Jamaica, NY 11434 USA
☎ (718) 712 1769
Fax 718/ 712 1574

Times to Call: 11am to 5pm
Type of Provider: Courier company
Areas of Specialty: Latin America and Europe

DESTINATIONS	SAMPLE ROUND TRIP FARE	STANDARD ECONOMY FARE	LENGTH OF STAY
Latin America:			
Buenos Aires	$480	$1,500	8 to 13 days
Caracas	$210	$198	6 or 7 days
Mexico City	$150	$566	flexible
Montevideo	$480	n/a	10 or 12 days
Rio de Janeiro	$480	$1,632	9 to 14 days
Santiago	$480	$1,500	8 or 9 days
Europe (service projected to begin in late 1994):			
Amsterdam	tba	$1,138	2 weeks
Brussels	tba	$1,470	2 weeks
Frankfurt	tba	$2,992	2 weeks
London	tba	$1,438	2 weeks
Madrid	tba	$1,170	2 weeks
Milan	tba	$1,248	2 weeks

Payment Methods: Cash, money order, certified check
Courier Duties on Return Trip: Yes
Minimum Age: 18 years
In Business Since: 1985
Recommended Advance Reservations: 6 to 12 weeks

Call to check on last-minute discounts. This company maintains a cancellation phone list, but you must have traveled for Air Facility once in order to qualify for the list. Contact Alex Palacio to book a courier flight.

Air Facility is expanding its service substantially. Prices and destinations were still being arranged at press time, but Station Manager Claudio Bacchi assures that, "we're going to cover a lot of Europe." Check with the company to get the most current information.

Air Facility maintains its own offices in the countries it serves. Other companies often contract with a local shipping company in each country. Bacchi believes that his arrangement results in better service for clients, and better treatment for couriers. When one of their couriers ran out of money during a bank closure in Caracas, the company actually loaned her money to help her through the crisis. They also keep a "black list" of unreliable couriers, so make sure you fulfill your obligations when you fly courier for them.

Cheap Tickets, Inc.

1247 Third Avenue
New York, NY 10021 USA
☎ (800) 377 1000, (212) 570 1179
Fax 800/ 454 2555

Times to Call: 9am to 11pm weekdays, 9am to 3pm Saturday
Type of Provider: Consolidator
Areas of Specialty: Hawaii, domestic USA, and international

DESTINATIONS	SAMPLE ROUND TRIP FARE	STANDARD ECONOMY FARE
Amsterdam	$339	$1,248
London	$349	$1,098
Los Angeles	$318	$700
Maui	$479	$1,280
Miami	$158	$598
Paris	$339	$1,360
Rome	$549	$1,298

Payment Methods: Cash, money order, certified check, personal check, Visa, MasterCard, American Express
In Business Since: 1986

Tickets are non-refundable and non-changeable unless specifically noted by Cheap Tickets. Additional offices in Hawaii, Los Angeles, Miami (opens late 1994), and San Francisco.

Consumer Wholesale Travel

34 West 33rd Street, Suite 1014
New York, NY 10001 USA
☎ (800) 223 6862, (212) 695 8435
Fax 212/ 695 8627

Times to Call: 9am to 5pm
Type of Provider: Consolidator
Areas of Specialty: India, Europe, Africa and around-the-world

DESTINATIONS	SAMPLE ROUND TRIP FARE	STANDARD ECONOMY FARE
Bombay	$840	$1,361
London	$299	$1,098
Johannesburg	$1,199	$2,670
Nairobi	$1,099	n/a
Paris	$399	$1,360
Tel Aviv	$699	$1,564

Payment Methods: Cash, personal check, Visa, MasterCard,
American Express
In Business Since: 1975

CWT frequently consolidates for Air France, British Airways, KLM, United, Virgin Atlantic, Virgin, and Air India. The company slogan is "best airlines at budget prices; buy today, fly tonight." They are Airline Reporting Corporation and Better Business Bureau members.

This is a very customer-friendly, personal operation run by a husband -and-wife team. Mina says, "our customers get married and have children, and we remember." Best of all, they will export tickets to anywhere in the world.

Council Travel

205 East 42nd Street
New York, NY 10017 USA
☎ (800) 743 1823, (212) 661 1450
Fax 212/ 682 0129

Times to Call: 9am to 5pm
Type of Provider: Discount travel agent
Areas of Specialty: Worldwide student, youth, and budget travel

DESTINATIONS	SAMPLE ROUND TRIP FARE	STANDARD ECONOMY FARE
Athens	$649	$2,040
Bangkok	$1,068	$1,533
London	$370	$1,098
San Jose	$450	$1,346
Tel Aviv	$718	$1,564

In Business Since: 1947

Payment Methods: Cash, money order, personal check, Visa, MasterCard

(See the Council Travel listing in the Chicago chapter for company background.)

Discount Travel International (DTI)

169 West 81st Street
New York, NY 10024 USA
☎ (800) FLY 4 DTI, (212) 362 3636
Fax 212/ 362 3236

Times to Call: 10am to 5:30pm
(Informational recording available after hours.)
Type of Provider: Courier booking agent, consolidator and standby broker
Areas of Specialty: Worldwide

DESTINATIONS	SAMPLE ROUND TRIP FARE	STANDARD ECONOMY FARE	LENGTH OF STAY
Courier flights:			
Buenos Aires	$520	$1,654	7 to 13 days
Brussels	$375	$1,470	7 to 21 days
Caracas	$250	$616	6 to 14 days
Hong Kong*	$500	$2,642	up to 2 mos.
London	$325	$1,098	7 to 8 days
Mexico City	$250	$630	3 to 30 days
Milan	$375	$1,248	9 days
Montevideo	$520	$1,654	15 days
San Juan	$250	$410	3 to 30 days
Rio de Janeiro	$525	$1,752	1 to 2 weeks
Santiago	$520	$1,654	1 week
Singapore*	$650	$3,300	7 to 30 days

New York	Sydney	$600	$4,814	up to 1 month
	Consolidated fares:			
	Amsterdam	$500	$1,248	
	Buenos Aires	$650	$1,654	
	Caracas	$525	$616	
	Chicago	$118	$498	
	Frankfurt	$460	$1,658	
	Los Angeles	$250	$700	
	Madrid	$479	$1,100	
	Miami	$150	$598	
	Paris	$425	$1,360	
	Rio de Janeiro	$650	$1,752	
	San Francisco	$250	$700	

Deposit: $100 for courier flights

Payment Methods: Cash, money order, certified check, Visa, MasterCard

Courier Duties on Return Trip: Yes

Minimum Age: 18 years

In Business Since: 1989

Recommended Advance Reservations: 2 to 3 months for courier flights

DTI offers the only toll-free telephone number in the courier business. one-way tickets are NOT available for courier flights. However, call to check on last-minute discounts on courier runs. DTI maintains a cancellation phone list. Some courier flights are on United Airlines, which permits couriers to check one bag. Ask about flights originating in Los Angeles, Miami, or San Francisco. DTI gets new consolidator and space-available destinations all the time, so call them to get the latest details. Space-available is the single cheapest way for flexible travelers to fly within the USA. Currently, most of these flights are on Wings of the World and Tower Air.

* Singapore and Hong Kong courier flights include a paid overnight stop in Tokyo.

East West Express

PO Box 30849

JFK Airport Station

Jamaica, NY 11430 USA

☎ (516) 561 2360

Fax 516/ 568 0477

Contact: Tracy

Times to Call: 9am to 5pm

(Informational recording available after hours.)

Type of Provider: Courier company

Areas of Specialty: Worldwide

DESTINATIONS	SAMPLE ROUND TRIP FARE	STANDARD ECONOMY FARE	LENGTH OF STAY
Bangkok	$650	$1,533	2 weeks
Hong Kong	$650	$2,642	2 weeks
Johannesburg	$1,050	$2,670	up to 45 days
Manila	$650	$1,321	2 weeks
Singapore	$650	$3,300	2 weeks
Sydney	$850	$4,814	7 to 90 days

Payment Methods: Cash, money order, certified check,

personal check

Courier Duties on Return Trip: Yes

Minimum Age: 18 years

In Business Since: 1989

Recommended Advance Reservations: 2 months

Call to check on last-minute discounts. The company will add a Los Angeles to Sydney run in late 1994.

Four Winds Travel

636 Broadway, Suite 10012

New York, NY 100 USA

☎ (212) 777 7637

Fax 212/ 777 7738

Times to Call: 9am to 5pm weekdays, 10am to 2pm Saturday

Type of Provider: Courier booking agent, discount travel agency, and standby broker

Areas of Specialty: Europe, Asia, domestic USA

Courier flights:

DESTINATIONS	SAMPLE ROUND TRIP FARE	STANDARD ECONOMY FARE	LENGTH OF STAY
Bangkok	$850	$1,533	Up to 55 days
Djakarta	$875	n/a	Up to 55 days
Papeete	$750	n/a	Up to 55 days
Singapore	$795	$3,300	Up to 55 days

DESTINATIONS	SAMPLE ROUND TRIP FARE	STANDARD ECONOMY FARE
Amsterdam	$330	$1,248
Chicago	$120	$498
Honolulu	$500	$1,180
London	$400	$1,098
Los Angeles	$198	$700
Paris	$400	$1,360
San Francisco	$198	$700

Deposit: $100 to $200

Payment Methods: Cash, money order, certified check, personal check

Courier Duties on Return Trip: Yes

Minimum Age: 18

In Business Since: 1988

Recommended Advance Reservations: 1 to 3 months for couriers, anytime for charters

Last-minute discounts are sometimes available. Four Winds is an affiliate of Way to Go Travel in Los Angeles. Prices increase slightly in summertime.

Some of their charter flights are booked on a "space-available" basis, which is why they are so cheap. There is some risk that you would not get on the plane on the date you specified, although the agency claims that a very high percentage of their space-available passengers board their first-choice flight. If you don't make it, you try again the next day. Tickets are non-refundable, but good for six months.

Halbart Express

147-05 176th Street
Jamaica, NY 11434 USA
☎ (718) 656 5000
Fax 718/ 244 0559

Times to Call: 10am to 3pm
(Informational recording available after hours.)
Type of Provider: Courier company
Areas of Specialty: Worldwide

DESTINATIONS	SAMPLE ROUND TRIP FARE	STANDARD ECONOMY FARE	LENGTH OF STAY
Copenhagen	$328	$1,890	1 week
Frankfurt	$328	$1,658	8 days
Hong Kong	$528	$2,642	7 to 21 days
Johannesburg	$975	$2,670	14 to 21 days
London	$278	$1,098	7 to 21 days
Madrid	$350	$1,100	7 to 21 days
Manila	$528	$1,321	7 to 21 days
Milan	$378	$1,248	7 or 14 days
Paris	$378	$1,360	1 week
Rio de Janeiro	$378	$1,752	1 week
Rome	$378	$1,298	8 days
Santiago	$350	$1,654	1 week
Seoul	$528	$2,744	7 to 21 days
Singapore	$528	$3,300	7 to 21 days
Stockholm	$328	$2,038	7 to 21 days
Tokyo	$528	$2,788	7 to 21 days

Deposit: $100
Payment Methods: Cash, money order, certified check, personal
check, Visa, MasterCard, American Express
Courier Duties on Return Trip: Yes
Minimum Age: 18 years
In Business Since: 1980
Recommended Advance Reservations: 1 to 3 months

Call to check on last-minute discounts. This company maintains a
cancellation phone list.

Couriers must meet at the office in Jamaica, New York, two hours prior to departure. By subway, get off the F-line at Parsons Boulevard, then catch the Q-113 bus to the Halbart office. The Halbart driver brings the courier and the mailbags to the airport.

Fares increase by about $100 near Thanksgiving, Christmas, and July through August.

Halbart offers courier flights departing from New York and Miami only. However, offices in Atlanta, Boston, Chicago, Detroit, Los Angeles, and Paris just may begin booking courier flights in 1995 or 1996.

Israpak Courier/Courier Network

295 Seventh Avenue
New York, NY 10001 USA
☎ (212) 684 7911

Times to Call: 7pm to 9pm only
Type of Provider: Courier company
Areas of Specialty: Israel

DESTINATIONS	SAMPLE ROUND TRIP FARE	STANDARD ECONOMY FARE	LENGTH OF STAY
Tel Aviv	$520	$1,564	1 day to 2 mos.

Payment Methods: Cash, money order, certified check, personal check, Visa, MasterCard
Courier Duties on Return Trip: Yes
Minimum Age: 18 years
In Business Since: 1989
Recommended Advance Reservations: 3 to 4 months

One-way tickets are available. In the winter, you can book a flight as little as two months in advance. Prices increase all the way up to $800 in July and August. Flights are on TWA, and couriers do earn frequent flier miles. The flight out takes a day and a half, and the return flight takes a full day, so it is best to plan to stay in Israel as long as possible. Couriers may bring one checked bag plus a carry-on.

Jupiter Air

Building No. 14
JFK International Airport
Jamaica, New York 11430 USA
☎ (718) 656 6050
Fax 718/ 656 7263
Contact: Marilyn or Migdalia to book your flight

Times to Call: 9am to 5pm
Type of Provider: Courier company
Areas of Specialty: Asia

DESTINATIONS	SAMPLE ROUND TRIP FARE	STANDARD ECONOMY FARE	LENGTH OF STAY
Hong Kong	$550	$2,642	7 to 30 days
London	$325	$1,098	7 to 30 days
Singapore	$550	$3,300	7 to 30 days

Annual Fee: $35 for 3 years
Deposit: $200
Payment Methods: Cash, money order, certified check,
personal check
Courier Duties on Return Trip: Yes
Minimum Age: 18 years
In Business Since: 1988
Recommended Advance Reservations: 0 to 3 months

Ask about last-minute discounts and the cancellation phone list.

Hong Kong is Jupiter Air's hub city. Thus it is sometimes possible to reserve a courier flight from Hong Kong to other Asian cities, such as Bangkok or Tokyo. Keep in mind that you must be back in Hong Kong in time for your return flight to San Francisco. The Hong Kong run includes one free night in a Tokyo hotel.

Additional offices in Hong Kong, Los Angeles, London, San Francisco, Seoul, Sydney, Taipei, and Tokyo. Jupiter strongly favors repeat business. Last-minute flights can be had for 50 percent off.

New Frontiers

12 East 33rd Street
New York, NY 10016 USA
☎ (800) 366 6387, (212) 779 0600
Fax 212/ 779 1006

Times to Call: 9am to 5pm
Type of Provider: Consolidator and charter operator
Areas of Specialty: Worldwide

DESTINATIONS	SAMPLE ROUND TRIP FARE	STANDARD ECONOMY FARE
Amsterdam	$558	$1,248
London	$398	$1,098
Nice	$578	$1,348
Paris	$398	$1,360
Rome	$678	$1,298

Payment Methods: Cash, money order, certified check, personal check, Visa, MasterCard, American Express
In Business Since: 1967

Discount tickets on Tower Air, American Trans Air, Continental, KLM, American Airlines, and CORSAIR. Started in 1967 by a French law student who was putting together a trip to Morocco for some friends, the entire trip cost a quarter of the price of a round trip air ticket from Paris to Casablanca. Later, he organized a second trip for 300 people, and Nouvelles Frontières (as the company is known in Europe) was born. They now have 132 offices worldwide, and some of the cheapest flights to or from the French-speaking world.

New Frontiers fought the airline cartel in a landmark 1985 case before the European Court of Justice, and won the right to sell discounted airfares.

Now Voyager

74 Varick Street, Suite 307
New York, NY 10013 USA
☎ (212) 431 1616
Fax 212/ 334 5243, 212/ 219 1753

Times to Call: 10am to 5:30pm weekdays, 12pm to 4:30pm
Saturday (Informational recording available from 6pm to 10am.)
Type of Provider: Courier broker, charter operator and standby broker
Areas of Specialty: Worldwide

DESTINATIONS	SAMPLE ROUND TRIP FARE	STANDARD ECONOMY FARE	LENGTH OF STAY
Bangkok	$689	$1,533	2 weeks
Copenhagen	$388	$1,890	1 week
Frankfurt	$388	$1,658	1 week
Hong Kong	$599	$2,642	7 to 21 days
Johannesburg	$999	$2,670	1 week
London	$409	$1,098	1 week
Madrid	$399	$1,100	1 week
Manila	$799	$1,321	2 weeks
Milan	$438	$1,248	11 or 14 days
Paris	$438	$1,360	1 week
Rio de Janeiro	$550	$1,752	1 week
Rome	$438	$1,298	8 days
Santiago	$450	$1,654	1 week
Seoul	$799	$2,744	2 weeks
Singapore	$750	$3,300	7 to 21 days
Stockholm	$388	$2,038	1 week
Sydney	$979	$4,814	1 week
Tokyo	$689	$2,788	7 to 21 days

Annual Fee: $50
Deposit: $100
Payment Methods: Cash, money order, certified check, personal
check, Visa, MasterCard, American Express
Courier Duties on Return Trip: Yes
Minimum Age: 18 years
In Business Since: 1984
Recommended Advance Reservations: 1 to 3 months

Call to check on last-minute discounts. Consolidator fares:
Amsterdam for $499. Ask about the last-minute phone list, called the
Jet-Setters Roster. They claim that 95 percent of standby customers
get onto their first flight. Now Voyager was founded by actress Julie
Weinberg.

Rush Courier, Inc.

481 49th Street
Brooklyn, NY 11220 USA
☎ (718) 439 8181
Fax 718/ 439 9043
Contact: Eileen

Times to Call: 10am to 4pm
Type of Provider: Courier company
Areas of Specialty: Puerto Rico

DESTINATIONS	SAMPLE ROUND TRIP FARE	STANDARD ECONOMY FARE	LENGTH OF STAY
San Juan	$200	$410	3 to 30 days

Payment Methods: Cash, money order, certified check, personal check.
Courier Duties on Return Trip: Yes
Minimum Age: 18 years
In Business Since: 1987
Recommended Advance Reservations: 2 to 3 months

One-way tickets to San Juan cost $150. Rush imposes a $25 cancellation fee. Call to check on last-minute discounts. This company maintains a cancellation phone list. Couriers are permitted two carry-ons only.

STA Travel

48 East 11th Street
New York, NY 10003 USA
☎ (800) 777 0112, (212) 477 7166
Fax 212/ 477 7348

Times to Call: 9am to 5pm
Type of Provider: Discount travel agency
Areas of Specialty: Worldwide

DESTINATIONS	SAMPLE ROUND TRIP FARE	STANDARD ECONOMY FARE
Amsterdam	$475	$1,248
Bangkok	$1,090	$1,533
Frankfurt	$525	$1,658
Hong Kong	$990	$2,642

			New York
London	$400	$1,098	
Singapore	$1,100	$3,300	
Sydney	$1,375	$4,814	
Tokyo	$795	$2,788	

Payment Methods: Cash, money order, certified check, personal check, Visa, MasterCard, American Express
In Business Since: 1975

STA is the world's largest travel organization for students and young, independent travelers. They have 120 locations worldwide. Some of their best fares require student ID, or carry a maximum age.

Their tickets are highly flexible, usually good for one year and requiring no advance purchase. Date changes can be made at any office worldwide for $25; refunds cost only $50 to $75. Such flexible tickets are a wise choice for travelers going on long trips without fully concrete itineraries. STA tickets are priced based on one-way tickets, which makes it easy to book open-jaw flights.

TFI Tours

34 West 32nd Street
New York, NY 10001 USA
☎ (800) 745 8000, (212) 736 1140
Fax 212/ 564 4081

Times to Call: 8:30am to 10pm weekdays, 9am to 8pm Saturday, 10am to 8pm Sunday
Type of Provider: Consolidator
Areas of Specialty: Worldwide

DESTINATIONS	SAMPLE ROUND TRIP FARE	STANDARD ECONOMY FARE
Amsterdam	$300	$1,248
Frankfurt	$380	$1,658
Johannesburg	$1,024	$2,670
London	$370	$1,098
Miami	$158	$598
Paris	$380	$1,360
Rio de Janeiro	$800	$1,752
Tokyo	$838	$2,788

Payment Methods: Cash, money order, certified check, Visa, MasterCard, American Express, Discover
In Business Since: 1982

TFI consolidates for 55 different airlines, including most of the major U.S. carriers. They sell to travel agents as well as the public.

Travac

989 Sixth Avenue
New York, NY 10018 USA
☎ (800) 872 8800

Times to Call: 8:30am to 8:30pm
Type of Provider: Nationwide consolidator
Areas of Specialty: Europe

DESTINATIONS	SAMPLE ROUND TRIP FARE	STANDARD ECONOMY FARE
Atlanta to Amsterdam	$620	$788
Miami to Amsterdam	$690	$1,138
Miami to Paris	$580	$1,696
New York to Paris	$530	$1,360
San Francisco to Frankfurt	$780	$2,294
San Francisco to London	$670	$1,498
San Francisco to Moscow	$960	$2,235

Payment Methods: Cash, money order, certified check, Visa, MasterCard
In Business Since: 1979

Consolidates for major airlines like Delta and Air France.

World Courier

137-42 Guy Brewer Boulevard
Jamaica, NY 11434 USA
☎ (718) 978 9552, (718) 978 9408
Fax 718/ 276 6932

Times to Call: 9am to 5pm
(Informational recording available after hours.)
Areas of Specialty: Worldwide

DESTINATIONS	SAMPLE ROUND TRIP FARE	STANDARD ECONOMY FARE	LENGTH OF STAY
Brussels	$300	$1,470	1 to 3 weeks
Mexico City	$200	$630	3 to 30 days
Milan	$300	$1,248	2 weeks

Payment Methods: Cash, money order, certified check, personal check, Visa, MasterCard, American Express
Courier Duties on Return Trip: No
Minimum Age: 18 years
In Business Since: 1980
Recommended Advance Reservations: 2 months

World uses New York area residents only, and couriers must hold a U.S. or EC passport. Couriers are allowed one piece of checked luggage on most flights.

The screening process at World is tougher than average. Call to request an application. Because their niche is premium courier services, they have to be very selective about whom they use to accompany their documents. In fact, they have been talking about using in-house couriers only, so PLEASE do follow your instructions carefully if you fly for them.

World has a great cancellation phone list, but you must have flown with them before in order to get on it. At the last-minute, you fly for free, and they pay the first night's hotel at your destination.

SAN FRANCISCO, USA

CHAPTER 7

MARKET TRENDS

San Francisco is a good jumping-off point for travel to the Pacific Rim. There is a healthy mix of discount, charter, and courier flights to Asia and Australia, and plenty of discount and charter opportunities to Europe. Courier flights to Europe are few and far between—you may find an occasional flight to London, but you will have to book far in advance. San Francisco is one of the best places in the world to buy an around-the-world or circle-Pacific ticket. Some consolidators will also sell tickets by mail to travelers flying between international points other than San Francisco. Most foreign tourists need an onward ticket to get into the United States.

STOPPING OVER IN SAN FRANCISCO

Dock-sitting Otis Redding was not the only visitor to find himself enamored with the City by the Bay. Condé Nast Traveler readers recently named San Francisco the Number One City Destination in the world. This scenic city actually holds a beauty contest of sorts, doling out the limited amount of new building permits only to developers who submit the most eye-pleasing designs.

San Francisco is a patchwork of neighborhoods, from the post-hippie **Haight-Ashbury**, to the yuppie **Pacific Heights**, to the trendy, industrial club district **South of Market (SoMa)**. The key to understanding San Francisco is to explore it one neighborhood at a time. "The City," as it is known by locals, is compact—a brisk 30-minute walk will take you from the waterfront, through **North Beach**, past **Chinatown**, the **Financial District**, and down to **Market Street**. The Muni bus and BART subway systems are cheap and convenient ways to get to the starting point for your walking adventures.

The center of the burgeoning San Francisco jazz scene is **Café du Nord**, at 2170 Market in the Castro [☎ (415) 861 5016]. The decor is upscale, yet the club draws a young, artsy crowd which is far too diverse (and far too hip) to categorize. Once a notorious speakeasy, du Nord now features some of the Bay Area's hottest jazz and blues acts, including rising star Lavay Smith and the Red Hot Skillet Lickers. Eat dinner there to get a cabaret table. More of a local secret is live

---

TELEPHONE COUNTRY CODE:

(1)

CURRENCY:
Dollar
US$1.00 = £0.62

---

salsa on Tuesdays. The Fabulous Juan offers free salsa lessons for novices at 9pm. At 10pm the curtain goes up and the live band goes on stage. No partners necessary.

Avoid the T-shirt-shop-infested-tourist-trap that is Fisherman's Wharf at all costs. The only exception to this rule is Pier 43 1/2, which is where you catch the Red and White ferries. On weekends, try brunch at the social, outdoor tables of **Sam's Anchor Café** [across the Golden Gate in Tiburon, ☎ (415) 435 4527]. The views from the Tiburon waterfront are great, but for true drama hike to the top of **Mount Tamalpais**. A less strenuous hike with pleasant views is the five-mile perimeter trail at **Angel Island State Park**. An oasis in the middle of the bay, Angel Island offers beaches, foraging deer, great picnic spots and historic buildings. Call the **Red and White Fleet** at (415) 546 2628 for more information and schedules for either destination.

CHEAP SLEEPS

The Globe Hostel
10 Hallam Place
San Francisco, CA 94103 USA
☎ (415) 431 0540

A hip crowd and well-designed common areas make this hostel a fun place to stay. The staff points out the most interesting of the SoMa clubs each night. The hostel serves breakfast and dinner, and features a sun roof, TV lounge, pool table, and a bar downstairs. The Globe does not take credit cards. Weekends, wander over to China Basin for outdoor brunches on the waterfront. My favorite, **The Ramp**, is at 855 China Basin, near the south end of 4th Street [☎ (415) 621 2378]. Local yachtsmen sail up to the restaurant to eat. Play your cards right, and you might even talk your way aboard as an extra deckhand.

Green Tortoise Guest House
494 Broadway
San Francisco, CA 94133 USA
☎ (415) 834 9060

The Green Tortoise Guest House's extremely central location makes it a great place from which to explore the City. It's on the edge of North Beach and Chinatown, half an hour or less from about anywhere by foot. Don't let the occasional strip joint fool you—this is a safe, up-and-coming neighborhood, with great food, cafés, and drinking establishments. Capacity is 85 people. Custom bunk beds give you lots of space in the rooms. Great showers and a sauna add to the appeal. Dorm rooms $14, singles $19.50, doubles $35. No curfew. Run by the Green Tortoise alternative bus people. They will be opening a bar/café/upscale billiards hall below the hostel, and plan to offer drink discounts to hostelers.

The San Francisco International Hostel (HI / AYH)
Building 240, Fort Mason
San Francisco, CA 94123 USA
☎ (415) 771 7277

There are great views of the sun setting under the Golden Gate Bridge, and rumor has it that the produce section of the nearby **Marina Safeway** supermarket is a great place to initiate interesting romantic relationships. Don't expect to meet a lot of people at the hostel itself, though. For some reason, the place is very quiet, and fails to encourage interactions between travelers. But the views from Fort Mason are remarkable. At $13 a night, this place is a bargain. Call two days ahead and book with a credit card, this hostel is always full in the summertime. Lights out at midnight, and lockout at 2am.

The Red Victorian
1665 Haight Street
San Francisco, CA 94117 USA
☎ (415) 864 1978

A casual, artistic and friendly atmosphere pervades this 18-room bed and breakfast, which is perched atop a family style breakfast nook and meditative art gallery. Outside the door is the eclectic, young population of the Upper Haight, who come to check out the alternative music and clothing stores in the area. The Red Vic is the only inn we know of that gives guided tours of its elaborately and individually decorated bathrooms. Experience a 25-year time warp in the summer of Love Room, or get cozy in the Teddy Bear Room. Rates start at $75 a night double, with shared bath. Continental breakfast in the

Global Village is included. Don't miss the tapas and sangria at **Cha Cha Cha** [1805 Haight, ☎ (415) 386 5758], just down the block. Or sprawl out on the pillows and sample inexpensive Mediterranean food at **Kan Zaman** [1793 Haight, ☎ (415) 751 9656]. Smoking the exotic tobacco hookas is extra, but watching the belly dancers is free. For unlimited daytime recreation possibilities, **Golden Gate Park** is but a short walk away. Clearly, the Red Vic has chosen an interesting neighborhood.

CHEAP EATS

There are lots of great Asian restaurants in Chinatown, where a meal will set you back only $3 to $5. One good bet is **Sam Woh's**, at 813 Washington [☎ (415) 982 0596]. Pop into **Wee On Co. Market**, directly across the street, if you fancy beer or wine with your dinner. Because the only beverage served at Sam Woh's is tea, jaywalking to Wee On has become a tradition.

For only a dollar more a plate, **House of Nanking's** spicy Chinese cuisine causes hour-long lines at lunch or dinner. Sizzling prawns and Nanking beef are quite popular, but Chef Fang even does wonderful things even with humble chow mein [919 Kearny at Colombus, ☎ (415) 421 1429]. Visit them at off-peak hours, or break up into groups of two. *The Zagat Survey* rates them among the top 25 restaurants in San Francisco, yet the bill won't exceed $9 a person.

In the Mission, **La Cumbre** [☎ (415) 863 8205] at 555 Valencia and 16th serves up some of the city's best burritos for $3.50; while you're in the neighborhood, step over to 647 Valencia for unpretentious beer, pool and dancing at the **Elbo Room** [☎ (415) 552 7788].

North Beach Pizza is another local favorite, with locations at 1310 and 1499 Grant Avenue [☎ (415) 433 2444]. At the **Bocce Café**, mix and match a dozen pastas with a dozen sauces for $5.95 a plate, in a pleasantly candle-lit atmosphere. They are also in North Beach, at 478 Green, near Grant [☎ (415) 981 2044].

TO & FROM THE AIRPORT

Take a shuttle bus from SFO airport to your doorstep (or vice-versa) for about $11; try SuperShuttle at [☎ (415) 558 8500]. By bus, the

SamTrans 7B and 7F buses [☎ (800) 660 4287] depart from the SamTrans sign on the upper level every 15 to 30 minutes. Forty minutes and exactly $1.25 later, you arrive at the downtown Transbay Terminal, at First and Mission, where you can catch a connecting Muni bus to anywhere in San Francisco.

UNIQUELY SAN FRANCISCO

Skip Fisherman's Wharf and Pier 39. Instead, catch a cable car (the Powell-Hyde line from Powell and Market Streets). Hop off at curvaceous **Lombard Street**, where you will enjoy a fabulous view of the City (when the fog is at bay). Then wander down Lombard to **Columbus Street**, where you can explore the old Italian neighborhood of North Beach. Follow the swirling aromas of garlic and espresso—Bohemian cafés, shops and eateries abound. Turn right at the Transamerica Pyramid to explore **Chinatown**.

For a different sort of adventure, tour **the Castro**, the slightly upscale hangout of San Francisco's strong gay and lesbian communities. To get there, take the Muni west on Market Street to Castro. The area's cafés, jazz clubs, and leather shops attract bustling crowds. Follow Castro Street as it turns into Divisadero, then head west on Haight to explore the equally infamous **Haight Ashbury**, home of dive bars and counterculture youth. The hippies have migrated, but the area is still lively, especially on weekends. Check with the **Visitor's Bureau** [☎ (415) 391 2000] for the dates of the **Haight Street Fair** and the **Castro Street Fair**, two summer festivals that bring out roughly 100,000 people.

Aereo Cut Throat Travel Outlet

731 Market Street, Suite 401
San Francisco, CA 94103 USA
☎ (800) 642 8747, (415) 989 8747
Fax 415/ 247 8737

Type of Provider: Consolidator
Areas of Specialty: Worldwide

DESTINATIONS	SAMPLE ROUND TRIP FARE	STANDARD ECONOMY FARE
Bangkok	$699	$1,452
London	$399	$1,498
Sydney	$719	$2,994
Tel Aviv	$819	$1,852

Payment Methods: Cash, money order, certified check, personal
check, Visa, MasterCard, American Express, wire transfer
In Business Since: 1987

In a 1992 *USA Today* test of travel agencies, Aereo offered the greatest savings of all consolidators polled, nationwide, on a flight from New York to London. By employing a specialist for each region of the world, Aereo claims to be better able to ferret out the very best deals for any destination. Aereo uses "local currency strategies" to take advantage of market discrepancies. Because of fluctuations in the international monetary system, sometimes it is cheaper to buy a ticket in your destination country's local market (and local currency) than to buy the translated price in your home currency.

Air Brokers International

323 Geary Street, Suite 411
San Francisco, CA 94102 USA
☎ (800) 883 3273, (415) 397 1383
Fax 415/ 397 4767

Times to Call: 9:15am to 5pm
Type of Provider: Consolidator
Areas of Specialty: Worldwide, especially around-the-world fares

DESTINATIONS	SAMPLE ROUND TRIP FARE	STANDARD ECONOMY FARE
Bali	$870	$1,818

94

Bangkok	$720	$1,452
London	$500	$1,498
Paris	$500	$1,900
Sydney	$800	$2,994
Tel Aviv	$900	$1,852

Payment Methods: Cash, money order, certified check, personal check, Visa, MasterCard, American Express
In Business Since: 1985

Frequently consolidates for Garuda, as well as Air France, Thai, Malaysian, China Air, Cathay Pacific, Qantas, EVA Airways, and Philippine Air.

Air Brokers' CEO is a high-energy man driven to find the cheapest fares available. Say you are flying to Greece. Are you going to visit a sailor? Because if you are (nudge-nudge, wink-wink), you can take advantage of Greece's special "seaman's fares," which automatically give you 15 percent off the lowest published fare.

Still, Air Brokers' specialty is constructing circle-Pacific and around-the-world fares. For example, fly Los Angeles–Hong Kong–Bangkok–Bali–Hawaii–Los Angeles for $949; or New York–Hong Kong–Bangkok–Delhi–Amsterdam/London–New York for $1,399. And should you need to purchase a ticket from outside the USA, give them a call.

AVIA Travel
5429 Geary Boulevard
San Francisco, CA 94121 USA
☎ (800) 950 2842, (415) 668 0964
Fax 415/ 386 8519

Times to Call: 9am to 5pm
Type of Provider: Discount travel agency
Areas of Specialty: Africa, Asia and around-the-world

DESTINATIONS	SAMPLE ROUND TRIP FARE	STANDARD ECONOMY FARE
Bangkok	$761	$1,452
London	$545	$1,498
Los Angeles	$98	$138

San Francisco	Paris	$745	$1,900
	Sydney	$920	$2,994
	Tel Aviv	$965	$1,852

Payment Methods: Cash, money order, certified check, personal check, Visa, MasterCard, American Express
In Business Since: 1986

AVIA's specialty is constructing circle-Pacific and around-the-world fares. For example, fly San Francisco–Taipei–Bangkok–Singapore–Djakarta–Bali–Hawaii–San Francisco for $1,090; or San Francisco–Taipei–Bangkok–Europe/London–San Francisco for $1,190.

Fax or write from abroad for exported discount tickets by mail. AVIA's focus on Asia enables them to get special deals on land packages as well.

Buenaventura Travel

595 Market Street, 22nd Floor
San Francisco, CA 94105 USA
☎ (800) 286 8872, (415) 777 9777
Fax 415/ 777 9871

Times to Call: 9am to 5pm
Type of Provider: Consolidator
Areas of Specialty: Latin America

DESTINATIONS	SAMPLE ROUND TRIP FARE	STANDARD ECONOMY FARE
Buenos Aires	$899	n/a
Guatemala	$570	$1,138
Lima	$780	n/a
Rio de Janeiro	$899	$2,166
San Jose	$570	$1,000
Santiago	$899	n/a

Payment Methods: Cash, money order, certified check, personal check, Visa, MasterCard, American Express
In Business Since: 1982

Prices are generally 15 to 20 percent off of APEX fares, often without advance purchase requirements that the airlines would impose.

Most fares are "common rated" (same price) for departures from either San Francisco or Los Angeles.

These IATA, ARC and Better Business Bureau members consolidate for the "main national carriers" of Central and South America. For countries where visas are necessary, they provide visa assistance for free. This Mom and Pop operation provides very personalized service. They'll even give you advice and maps for various cities and expeditions .

Char-Tours

562 Mission Street, Suite 500
San Francisco, CA 94105 USA
☎ (800) 323 4444, (415) 495 8881
Fax 800/ 388 8838, 415/ 543 8010

Type of Provider: Consolidator
Areas of Specialty: Europe and Middle East

DESTINATIONS	SAMPLE ROUND TRIP FARE	STANDARD ECONOMY FARE
Athens	$760	n/a
London	$555	$1,498
Milan	$695	$1,874
Moscow	$775	$2,235
Paris	$410	$1,900
Tel Aviv	$955	$1,852
Zurich	$675	$2,136

In Business Since: 1957
Payment Methods: Cash, personal check, Visa, MasterCard

Booking agents for New Frontiers' charter airline Corsair. Also consolidates for a variety of major scheduled airlines.

Sister company Empire Tours specializes in air and land packages to Hawaii, the Bahamas, and Mexico on Hawaiian Air and Northwestern. In shoulder season they will sell airfare without hotel if you rent a car for a minimum of two days.

Char-Tours books departures from airports across the country, but all flights are booked through the toll-free number at the San Francisco address.

Offers a few flights to the Pacific Rim and to Latin America, but no domestic flights whatsoever.

Cheap Tickets, Inc.

1230 El Camino Real, Suite L
San Bruno, CA 94066 USA
☎ (800) 377 1000, (415) 588 3700
Fax 800/ 454 2555

Times to Call: 6am to 8pm weekdays, 9am to 3pm Saturday
Type of Provider: Consolidator
Areas of Specialty: Hawaii, domestic USA, and international

DESTINATIONS	SAMPLE ROUND TRIP FARE	STANDARD ECONOMY FARE
Bangkok	$889	$1,452
London	$630	$1,498
Maui	$309	$1,068
Paris	$779	$1,900
Sydney	$799	$2,994
Tokyo	$589	$2,038

Payment Methods: Cash, money order, certified check, personal check, Visa, MasterCard, American Express
In Business Since: 1986

Tickets are non-refundable and non-changeable unless specifically noted by Cheap Tickets. Additional offices in Hawaii, Los Angeles, Miami (opens late 1994), and New York.

Council Travel

530 Bush Street
San Francisco, CA 94108 USA
☎ (800) 743 1823, (415) 421 3473
Fax 415/ 421 5603

Times to Call: 9am to 5pm
Type of Provider: Discount travel agent
Areas of Specialty: Worldwide student, youth, and budget travel

DESTINATIONS	SAMPLE ROUND TRIP FARE	STANDARD ECONOMY FARE
Bali	$979	$1,818
Bangkok	$768	$1,452
London	$568	$1,498
New York	$298	$700
Sydney	$925	$2,994
Tel Aviv	$818	$1,852

In Business Since: 1947

Payment Methods: Cash, money order, personal check, Visa, MasterCard

Open from 10am to 2pm Saturdays, for walk-in clients only.

(See the Council Travel listing in the Chicago chapter for company background.)

Discount Travel International (DTI)

169 West 81st Street
New York, NY 10024 USA
☎ (800) FLY 4 DTI, (212) 362 3636
Fax 212/ 362 3236

Times to Call: 10am to 5:30pm
(Informational recording available after hours.)
Type of Provider: Courier booking agent, consolidator and standby-broker
Areas of Specialty: Worldwide

DESTINATIONS	SAMPLE ROUND TRIP FARE	STANDARD ECONOMY FARE	LENGTH OF STAY
Bangkok	$425	$1,452	7 to 15 days
London	$425	$1,498	up to 14 days
Manila	$520	$1,624	7 to 30 days
Singapore	$500	$2,552	7 to 30 days
Consolidated fares:			
Chicago	$125	$650	
New York	$125	$700	
Paris	$500	$1,900	

Deposit: $100 for courier flights
Payment Methods: Cash, money order, certified check, Visa,

MasterCard
Courier Duties on Return Trip: Yes
Minimum Age: 18 years
In Business Since: 1989
Recommended Advance Reservations: 2 to 3 months for courier flights

We commend DTI for offering the only toll-free telephone number in the courier business. All DTI departures are booked through their New York office.

One-way tickets are NOT available for courier flights. However, call to check on last-minute discounts on courier runs. DTI maintains a cancellation phone list. Some courier flights are on United Airlines, which permits couriers to check one bag. Ask about flights originating in Los Angeles, Miami, or New York. DTI gets new consolidator and space-available destinations all the time, so call them to get the latest details. Space-available is the single cheapest way for flexible travelers to fly within the USA. Currently, most of these flights are on Wings of the World and Tower Air.

Singapore and Hong Kong courier flights include a paid overnight stop in Tokyo.

IBC Pacific (International Bonded Courier)

1595 El Segundo Blvd.
El Segundo, CA 90245 USA
☎ (310) 607 0125
Fax 310/ 607 0126

Times to Call: 9am to 4pm Tuesday through Friday
Type of Provider: Courier company
Areas of Specialty: Pacific Rim

DESTINATIONS	SAMPLE ROUND TRIP FARE	STANDARD ECONOMY FARE	LENGTH OF STAY
Bangkok	$475	$1,452	7 to 18 days

Deposit: $500!
Payment Methods: Cash, money order, certified check, personal check
In Business Since: 1988

Luggage: Carry-on only
Courier Duties on Return Trip: Yes
Recommended Advance Reservations: 6 to 8 weeks
Minimum Age: 21 years

IBC books its San Francisco courier flights through agents at its Los Angeles office.

Jupiter Air

90 South Spruce Avenue #1
South San Francisco, CA 94080 USA
☎ (415) 872 0845
Fax 415/ 871 4975
Contact: Hayley Liu or Kathie Po

Times to Call: 9am to 5pm
Type of Provider: Courier company
Areas of Specialty: Asia

DESTINATIONS	SAMPLE ROUND TRIP FARE	STANDARD ECONOMY FARE	LENGTH OF STAY
Bangkok	$330	$1,452	7 to 30 days
Hong Kong	$480	$1,892	7 to 30 days
★ London	$300	$1,498	7 to 30 days ★
Manila	$455	$1,624	7 to 30 days
Singapore	$435	$2,552	7 to 30 days

[handwritten: 30 days p. 135 -136 London - Rome]

Annual Fee: $35 for 3 years
Deposit: $200
Payment Methods: Cash, money order, certified check, personal check
Courier Duties on Return Trip: Yes
Minimum Age: 18 years
In Business Since: 1988
Recommended Advance Reservations: 0 to 3 months

Ask about last-minute discounts (50 percent off) and the cancellation phone list.

Hong Kong is Jupiter Air's hub city. Thus it is sometimes possible to reserve a courier flight from Hong Kong to other Asian cities, such as Bangkok or Tokyo. Keep in mind that you must be back in Hong Kong in time for your return flight to San Francisco.

Additional offices in Hong Kong, London, Los Angeles, New York, Seoul, Sydney, Taipei, Tokyo. Jupiter strongly favors repeat business. Last-minute flights can be had for 50 percent off.

Piece of Mind Travel

1028 Folsom Street
San Francisco, CA 94103 USA
☎ (415) 864 1995
Fax 415/ 864 2280
Contact: Rahn

Times to Call: 11am to 6pm
Type of Provider: Consolidator and standby broker
Areas of Specialty: Domestic USA and Europe

DESTINATIONS	SAMPLE ROUND TRIP FARE	STANDARD ECONOMY FARE
Amsterdam	$235*	$1,468
Chicago	$250	$650
Kingston	$198	$796
Maui	$260	$1,068
Miami	tba	$719
New York	$250	$700
Paris	$550	$1,900

Payment Methods: Cash, money order, traveler's check
In Business Since: 1994

*The Amsterdam flight is one-way only. Refer to the Amsterdam chapter to book your return flight.

Piece of Mind is the only company in San Francisco that books "space-available" flights. There is some risk that you may not get on the plane on the date you specify, although the agency claims that 90 percent of their standby passengers board their first-choice flight. If you don't get on the flight, you try again the next day. Confirmed seats are sometimes available for $100 more.

STA Travel

51 Grant Avenue
San Francisco, CA 94108 USA
☎ (800) 777 0112, (415) 391 8407
Fax 415/ 391 4105

Times to Call: 9am to 5pm
Type of Provider: Discount travel agency
Areas of Specialty: Worldwide

DESTINATIONS	SAMPLE ROUND TRIP FARE	STANDARD ECONOMY FARE
Amsterdam	$660	$1,468
Bangkok	$825	$1,452
Frankfurt	$735	$2,294
Hong Kong	$730	$1,892
London	$515	$1,498
Singapore	$845	$2,552
Sydney	$1,065	$2,994
Tokyo	$615	$2,038

Payment Methods: Cash, money order, certified check, personal
check, Visa, MasterCard, American Express
In Business Since: 1975

STA is the world's largest travel organization for students and young,
independent travelers. They have 120 locations worldwide. Some of
their best fares require student ID, or carry a maximum age.

Their tickets are highly flexible, usually good for one year and requiring no advance purchase. Date changes can be made at any office
worldwide for $25; refunds cost only $50 to $75. Such flexible tick-
ets are a wise choice for travelers going on long trips without fully
concrete itineraries. STA tickets are priced based on one-way tickets,
which makes it easy to book open-jaw flights.

SunTrips

The SunTrips Building
2350 Paragon Drive
San Jose, CA 95131 USA
☎ (800) 786 8747, (408) 432 1101

Times to Call: 7:30am to 6:30pm weekdays, 9am to 4pm Saturday
Type of Provider: Charter operator
Areas of Specialty: Europe, Mexico and domestic USA

DESTINATIONS	SAMPLE ROUND TRIP FARE	STANDARD ECONOMY FARE
Boston	$218	$734
Cancun	$229	$912
Honolulu	$219	$918
London	$398	$1,498
Mexico City	$189	$556
New York	$218	$700

Payment Methods: Cash, money order, certified check, personal check, Visa, MasterCard, American Express
In Business Since: 1976

SunTrips' coast-to-coast and London flights operate in spring and summer only, except for the Los Angeles to Boston run.

Hawaii and coast-to-coast flights are scheduled service. Mexico and London are charter flights. London flights use Stansted Airport, which has a direct rail link to the London Underground's Liverpool Station. Most aircraft are provided and operated by Leisure Air, a major charter company.

TFI Tours

760 Market Street, Suite 559
San Francisco, CA 94102 USA
☎ (800) 745 8000, (415) 441 3330
Fax 212/ 564 4081

Times to Call: 8:30am to 10pm weekdays, 9am to 8pm Saturday, 10am to 8pm Sunday
Type of Provider: Consolidator
Areas of Specialty: Worldwide

DESTINATIONS	SAMPLE ROUND TRIP FARE	STANDARD ECONOMY FARE
Bangkok	$800	$1,452
Frankfurt	$700	$2,294
London	$580	$1,498
Los Angeles	$770	$138

Paris	$710	$1,900
Rio de Janeiro	$310	$2,166
Tokyo	$590	$2,038

Payment Methods: Cash, money order, certified check, Visa, MasterCard, American Express, Discover
In Business Since: 1982

TFI consolidates for 55 different airlines, including most of the major U.S. carriers. They sell to travel agents as well as the public.

Travel Time

1 Halladie Plaza, Suite 406
San Francisco, CA 94102 USA
☎ (800) 956 9327, (415) 677 0799
Fax 415/ 391 1856

Times to Call: 9am to 5:30pm, 10am to 2pm Saturday
Type of Provider: Discount Travel Agency
Areas of Specialty: Mexico, Hawaii, and Europe, including around-the-world

DESTINATIONS	SAMPLE ROUND TRIP FARE	STANDARD ECONOMY FARE
Amsterdam	$621	$1,468
Cancun	$269	$912
Honolulu	$219	$918
London	$600	$1,498
Maui	$239	$1,068
Mexico City	$219	$556

Payment Methods: Cash, personal check, Visa, MasterCard, American Express
In Business Since: 1983

Travel Time focuses on a few areas, rather than doing the whole world. Agents are specialists in a particular region, and are actually paid to visit their areas of expertise each year.

They also specialize in around-the-world, circle-Pacific, and other customized multi-stop itineraries. They can issue tickets originating and terminating anywhere in the world. Fax or e-mail (ehasbrouck @igc.apc.org) to save telephone charges from outside the USA.

UTL Travel

320 Corey Way
South San Francisco, CA 94080 USA
☎ (415) 583 5074
Fax 415/ 583 8122
Contact: Grace or Iris

Times to Call: 9am to 6pm
Type of Provider: Courier booking agent
Areas of Specialty: Asia

DESTINATIONS	SAMPLE ROUND TRIP FARE	STANDARD ECONOMY FARE	LENGTH OF STAY
Hong Kong	tba	$1,892	14 to 30 days
Manila	$405	$1,624	14 to 30 days
Singapore	$385	$2,552	14 to 30 days

Deposit: $100 to $200
Payment Methods: Cash, money order, certified check
Luggage: Varies by destination
In Business Since: 1988
Recommended Advance Reservations: 2 to 3 months

Prices increase by $50 in June, July, August and December. UTL offers both last-minute discounts and a cancellation phone list. They are the booking agents for TNT Skypak and Jupiter Air.

America's Low-Fare Airlines

Americans are always complaining about how high domestic airfares are. Far too often, I hear people say things like, "I could fly to Europe for less than they want to charge me for this domestic flight!" Good old Southwest Airlines has done a great job of making domestic flights cheap again. In fact, they have been so successful, they have spawned a whole new category: low-fare airlines. Their prices are often less than half of the lowest fares charged by the major airlines. In fact, when the low-fare airlines and the majors offers the same fare on the same route, we fly the low-fare airline. We know that when a low-fare carrier starts a new route, the major airlines usually match the lower fare for a few seats on each plane. If the upstarts leave a market, the fares go back up. So support the little guys.

CHAPTER 8

As these upstarts are proving, charging a fair price is more important than having a big name. This is especially true when tickets are purchased by small companies and vacationers. The public seems most receptive to "no-frills" flights on short hops, which don't last long enough for anyone to start feeling too deprived. In fact, the traveling public has responded quite favorably to the new carriers. Significant increases in passenger traffic have been noted in most low-fare markets. Where people once drove, took the train, or simply did not make the trip, they are now taking advantage of the low fares and are traveling by plane.

The following section gives you a rundown of the low-fare airline line-up.

American Trans Air
☎ (800) 225 2995

First Flight: 1973
Based: Indianapolis

ATA runs charter planes, which it fills by selling seats directly to passengers as well as by selling to tour operators. The charter operation gives ATA the flexibility to move into (and out of) markets quickly, taking advantage of trends before the majors can make adjustments. Service runs from the West Coast to Chicago, Indianapolis, and New York, as well as to Belfast, Cancun, Nassau, and Riga. The airline was founded by a Latvian immigrant who started with a single plane. Their peak season runs from December through April, which leads to some particularly good deals in the summer months. One caveat: ATA's seats are as cramped as its prices are low. Sample fare: San Francisco to New York for $378 round trip.

Kiwi International Airlines
☎ (800) 538 5494

First Flight: 1992
Based: Newark, New Jersey

Employee-owned Kiwi was started by former Pan Am and Eastern Airlines workers. Pilots put in $50,000 a piece, and other employees contributed $5,000 each. When Continental tried to crush the fledgling Kiwi with a fare war, its employee/owners agreed to a 50 percent pay cut for everyone except single parents. They used the savings to buy cut fares, and were able to beat back Continental's challenge. Its hubs at Newark and Chicago Midway serve Atlanta, Puerto Rico, and various Florida sunspots. Kiwi has its own frequent flier program. Changes cost $25, and cancellations are $50. There are no advance-purchase or minimum-stay requirements, but you must book early to get the lowest-priced, capacity-controlled seats. Food and leg room are above average. Sample fare: Newark to West Palm Beach for $164.

MarkAir
☎ (800) 627 5247

First Flight: 1947
Based: Anchorage, Alaska, with hubs in Denver and Seattle

This no-frills carrier recently yanked out all of its first-class seating to make more room for coach passengers. Its territory ranges from Alaska to San Diego, and from the Pacific to the Atlantic. Its strategy of offering only one or two flights per day between a score of cities across the U.S. is unusual. The idea is to avoid taking so much traffic away from the majors that they provoke massive retaliatory fare-wars. Seating is tight, and there are no meals. Sample fare: Seattle to Dallas for $199 one-way.

Midway Airlines

☎ (800) 446 4392

First Flight: 1993
Based: Chicago's Midway Airport

Its predecessor having gone bankrupt in 1991, this Midway was started by new investors in 1993. Its routes run from Chicago to Dallas, Denver, New York (LaGuardia), Philadelphia, and Washington, D.C. Fares vary slightly depending on refundability, seven-day advance purchase, and Saturday night stay. Seating is better than average. You get a free flight every 10,000 miles, or you can use your miles on American or United. Sample fare: New York to Chicago for $99 each way.

Midwest Express

☎ (800) 452 2022

First Flight: 1984
Based: Milwaukee

This company's angle might just catch on: they offer near-First Class service at coach prices. On DC-9s where most airlines would install five seats per row, Midwest Express has only four. They also use cloth napkins and offer free wine on all flights. Frequent flier miles can also be used on Air New Zealand, Scandinavian Airlines, and Virgin Atlantic. This company was born as the in-house airline for Kimberly-Clark business travelers. Routes extend to both coasts from Milwaukee. The cheapest flights are non-refundable, require a Friday or Saturday night stay, and require a 14-day advance purchase. Sample fare: Milwaukee to Los Angeles round trip for $298.

National Air

☎ (800) 949 9400

First Flight: 1993
Based: Atlanta

Formerly Private Jet, this ambitiously named carrier is better known for its charter flights. National's scheduled service connects the Midwest, Florida, Texas and the West. Seats are very tight, and are cheaper with a 7-day advance purchase. Its one-stop transcontinental fares are a good deal. Sample fare: Atlanta to Las Vegas for $159 each way.

Reno Air
☎ (800) RENO 247

First Flight: 1992
Based: Reno

Like many of the major airlines, Reno uses a hub-and-spoke system. Its hubs in Reno, Nevada and San Jose, California, serve the western United States. Flights range from San Diego to Seattle. The product is billed as full service at a low price. The fare structure favors 14-day and 7-day advance purchases over walk-ups. Also, their first class service is a great value. Their low-key management style keeps employees happy, and makes the carrier fun to fly. Reno Air flights earn mileage on American Airlines' frequent flier program. Sample fare: San Jose to Las Vegas for $52 each way.

Southwest Airlines
☎ (800) I FLY SWA

First Flight: 1971
Based: Dallas

The pioneer in low-fare, short hop flights, Southwest's strategy has been to lure passengers off the highways by making flying and driving competitive in price. During one fare war, Southwest was charging $19 each way from Cleveland to Baltimore, when the bus fare between the same cities was $44. They serve snacks instead of meals, and their frequent flier miles cannot be used on other carriers, but at these prices, no one is complaining. Also, they service planes and get them back in the air faster than anyone else in the business. Southwest recently purchased Morris Air, which runs an incredibly similar operation in the Rocky Mountains region. *USA Today* has estimated that Southwest influences one-third of all domestic airfares. Sample fare: San Francisco to Los Angeles for $49.

Tower Air

☎ (800) 34 TOWER

First Flight: 1984

Based: JFK Airport, New York

Tower is unique among the low-fare carriers in that it focuses on longer flights, competing directly with the profit centers of the major airlines. From New York, flights service Los Angeles, Miami, San Francisco and San Juan, as well as Amsterdam, Dublin, New Delhi, Paris, Sao Paulo, and Tel Aviv. Business class costs only $75 more than coach on most flights. There are no restrictions, and no meals. Seats are much more comfortable than average. However, the Department of Transportation reports that Tower had more consumer complaints than any other national carrier during the first quarter of 1994 (eight complaints per 100,000 passengers, which is still not bad). Sample fare: New York to San Francisco for $149 each way.

ValuJet

☎ (800) 825 8538

First Flight: 1993

Based: Atlanta

ValuJet promotes an informal, no-frills image. Most of its flights are in the Southeast, but range from Philadelphia and Chicago to Miami and Dallas. Their fare structure has three levels: the cheapest is for 21-day advance purchases, next best is 7-day advance, and still good is the walk-up fare. Tickets are non-refundable, but carry no odd restrictions. Actually, paper tickets as such are never even issued. ValuJet uses an advanced electronic booking system, and gives each passenger a confirmation number instead of a ticket. Sample fare: Atlanta to Jacksonville one-way for $39 with a 21-day advance purchase, or $89 as a walk-up fare.

Wings of the World

☎ (800) U FLY WOW

First Flight: 1991

Based: Los Angeles

WOW, as I like to think of it, is actually a charter operator, selling seats

111

mostly on American Trans Air planes. They offer regularly scheduled, low-fare, point to point flights to a variety of destinations in the U.S. and abroad. There are no minimum stay requirements, but a 7-day advance purchase is required for the cheapest fares. In the U.S., WOW serves Chicago, Honolulu, Los Angeles, New York, and San Francisco. Internationally, they fly from major U.S. cities to Paris and Mexico City. Sample fare: Los Angeles to Paris for $498 round trip.

AMSTERDAM, THE NETHERLANDS

MARKET TRENDS

Amsterdam is well-known for its consolidators. The famously permissive government lets agencies sell tickets for well below IATA fares. Amsterdam is particularly good for intra-European travel. For flights to other continents, the cheapest flights are still in London. Citizens of most of Asia, Africa, Eastern Europe, and Latin America need both visas and onward tickets in order to enter the country.

STOPPING OVER IN AMSTERDAM

Amsterdam has maintained a penchant for the exotic ever since 17th-century Dutch explorers returned with such interesting novelties as tobacco, porcelain, coffee, and rare spices. The spicy Indonesian rijsttafel ("rice table") was one of these wonderful imports, and is now a culinary must for those visiting the Netherlands.

As you might expect, canals and the harbor play a big part in the feel of this city, much of which is built below sea level. Tranquil strolls along the canals are in order, as is the panoramic harbor view seen on the ferry ride from Centraal Station to Amsterdam Noord.

Whether out of political expedience or respect for individual liberties, the Netherlands has some of the most permissive vice laws in the western world. Both soft drug use and prostitution are tolerated by the authorities. While you won't see large marijuana leaves painted on the doors of the cafés anymore (they've been replaced by green ferns in the window), the substance is still for sale inside. Absolutely avoid transporting any such substance outside of the country—foreign customs agents use dogs on the trains and buses leaving the Netherlands. The red-light district is another anomaly in western society. Lingerie-clad prostitutes pose in the windows of houses along canal-lined streets, as locals, tourists, and even couples stroll past. The area is said to be safe, probably due to the presence of voyeuristic crowds who seem driven to see this for themselves. Ironically, the district surrounds Oude Kerk, the city's oldest Gothic church.

Summertime is a great time to check out **Vondelpark**. The Dutch answer to New York's Central Park, the park was one giant camp-

TELEPHONE COUNTRY CODE:
(31)

CURRENCY:
Guilder
US$1.00 = f1.60

113

ground for flower children in the Sixties. Nowadays, the campers have been replaced by street artists, who give way to regular concerts and plays in the open-air theater all summer long. If you are looking for quiet, escape into the wooded glens and lakes surrounding the theater. Visitors may want to stop for tea at the avantgarde **Ronde Blauwe Theehuis**, or relax at the terrace café of the nearby **Filmmuseum**.

A wide variety of nightlife options, from quiet chess cafés to roudy punk performances, keep the local scene interesting. Popular among both travelers and locals is the **Melkweg**, or Milky Way. This unique venue hosts art events, films, theater, poetry readings, and (especially on weekends) live bands.

CHEAP SLEEPS

Bob's Youth Hostel

NZ Voorburgwal 92

☎ (020) 623 00 63

An Amsterdam institution, Bob's downstairs café has been the meeting point for tens of thousands of backpack-toting explorers. A fun place to socialize, the café is also a good place for a cheap meal. Upstairs, clean, single-sex dorm beds run f20 a night. 3am curfew.

Sleep In

's-Gravesandestraat 51-53

☎ (020) 694 74 44

When everything else in town is full for the night, you can turn to this mega-hostel for help. Bunks in 100-person rooms go for f14, breakfast is f5 extra. Live bands and flower children are seen here frequently. No curfew. Metro: Weesperplein.

Hotel van Onna

Bloemgracht 102

☎ (020) 626 58 01

Moving up a notch in price, the clean rooms go for f60 a person, in singles through quads. The pleasant, older Jordaan neighborhood has more cafés than tourists. Enjoy your breakfast and your view of the canal, and venture out with the hordes only when you are good and ready. Reservations recommended. Tram: No. 13 or 17 from Centraal Station.

CHEAP EATS

Stalls at the Waterlooplein flea market purvey some of the cheapest eats in the city. However, **Anno Vleminckx Sausmeesters** (Voetboogstraat 33) gives the stalls stiff competition, serving up overflowing paper cones of French fries with sauce for f2. Pancakes are a traditional Dutch supper item, and can be picked up at any of several dozen shops for under f10.

For great rijsttafel on a budget, head over to the Leidseplein. **Bojo**, at Lange Leidsedwarstr. 51, has various Indonesian specialties, including rijsttafel, for about f16 a person. Open until 2am weeknights, until 5am on Friday and Saturday.

TO & FROM THE AIRPORT

Netherlands Railways operates very frequent service from the basement of Amsterdam Schiphol Airport to the Central Station (16 minutes) for f4.50. You must purchase your ticket before boarding. For those seeking convenience over savings, the KLM Shuttle bus departs twice hourly from Schiphol, stopping at each of the major downtown hotels. The fare is f20, payable to the driver, and the ride lasts 20 to 50 minutes.

UNIQUELY AMSTERDAM

Amsterdam is so bicycle-friendly that you can ride from Centraal Station to the city's edge in half an hour. You will be amazed at how abruptly the city ends and the farmhouses and countryside begin. The surrounding area's many lakes and ponds lend it the name Waterland. To get there, take your rented bicycle back behind the station to catch the free ferry across the IJ. Then follow Buiksloterweg, turn right at Café Trefpunt, and follow the signs towards Nieuwendam. You can follow the coastline to Uitdam (6 km from Amsterdam), and then turn inland towards the village Broek in Waterland (6km further). Those inspired by the ride can continue another hour north to **Edam** (home of the cheese), while those who have satisfied their needs already can stop for the traditional post-ride pancake at **De Witte Swaen**. The Broek trip takes about three hours, while the Edam trip requires about five.

European Travel Network

Damrak 30
Amsterdam, NETHERLANDS
☎ (020) 622 6473
Fax 020/ 638 2271

Times to Call: 9am to 5pm
Type of Provider: Consolidator
Areas of Specialty: Asia, Africa, Latin America, Australia, North America

DESTINATIONS	SAMPLE ROUND TRIP FARE	STANDARD ECONOMY FARE
Delhi	f1,099	f5,584
Nairobi	f1,138	f6,579
Rio de Janeiro	f1,425	f8,276
Singapore	f1,245	f6,925
Sydney	f2,045	f4,512

Payment Methods: Cash, money order, certified check, personal check
In Business Since: 1974

They book flights for everywhere in the world except Europe.

Future Line Travel

Prof. Tulpplein 4
Amsterdam, NETHERLANDS
☎ (020) 622 2859
Fax 020/ 639 0199

Times to Call: 9am to 5pm
Type of Provider: Consolidator
Areas of Specialty: Worldwide

DESTINATIONS	SAMPLE ROUND TRIP FARE	STANDARD ECONOMY FARE
Bangkok	f1,290	f2,866
London	f393	f576
Los Angeles	f1,247	f5,751
New York	f690	f4,066
Sydney	f2,273	f4,512
Tel Aviv	f999	f3,715

Payment Methods: Cash, Visa, American Express, Eurocard

In Business Since: 1986

Future Line can ship tickets to buyers in other countries, with a surcharge of f25. Youth hostel members receive a discount on the ferries to England. Also, Future Line can book youth hostels via their computer system.

NBBS Reizen

Haarlemmerstraat 115

1013EM Amsterdam NETHERLANDS

☎ (020) 626 2557

Fax 071/ 22 64 75

Times to Call: 9:30am to 5:30pm

Type of Provider: Discount travel agency

Areas of Specialty: Worldwide

DESTINATIONS	SAMPLE ROUND TRIP FARE	STANDARD ECONOMY FARE
Athens	f595	f3,138
Bangkok	f1,170	f2,866
Djakarta	f1,430	f3,266
London	f280	f576
Los Angeles	f1,195	f5,751
New York	f592	f4,066
Rome	f445	f2,299
Sydney	f1,980	f4,512

Payment Methods: Cash, bank transfer

In Business Since: 1975

Member of the STA Travel Network. STA is the world's largest travel organization for students and young, independent travelers. They have 120 locations worldwide. Some of their best fares require student ID, or carry a maximum age.

Their tickets are highly flexible, usually good for one year and requiring no advance purchase. Date changes can be made at any office worldwide for $25; refunds cost only $50 to $75. Such flexible tickets are a wise choice for travelers going on long trips without fully concrete itineraries. STA tickets are priced based on one-way tickets, which makes it easy to book open-jaw flights.

Sister company Budget Air [☎ (020) 627 1251] does accept credit cards for the purchase of discount air travel, but cannot make changes on STA tickets.

Near East Tours

9–15 Rokin Straat
1012KK Amsterdam, NETHERLANDS
☎ (020) 624 3350
Fax 0020/ 627 8641

Times to Call: 9am to 5pm
Type of Provider: Consolidator
Areas of Specialty: Israel

DESTINATIONS	SAMPLE ROUND TRIP FARE	STANDARD ECONOMY FARE
Tel Aviv	f 649	f3,715

Payment Methods: Cash, money order, certified check, personal check
In Business Since: 1961

This company specializes in tour packages to Israel, but also sells air only.

Nouvelles Frontières

1 Van Baerlestraat #3
1071 A1 Amsterdam NETHERLANDS
☎ (020) 664 0447
Fax 020/ 675 3457

Times to Call: 9am to 5pm
Type of Provider: Consolidator and charter operator
Areas of Specialty: Worldwide

DESTINATIONS	SAMPLE ROUND TRIP FARE	STANDARD ECONOMY FARE
Bangkok	f1,250	f2,866
Dakar	f1,200	f4,650
Delhi	f1,095	f5,584

| *Amsterdam* | London | f220 | f576 |
| | Paris | f300 | f986 |

Payment Methods: Cash, money order, certified check, personal
check, Visa, MasterCard, American Express
In Business Since: 1967

Discount tickets on Tower Air, American Trans Air, Continental, KLM,
American Airlines, and CORSAIR.

Started in 1967 by a French law student who was putting together a
trip to Morocco for some friends. The entire trip cost a quarter of the
price of a round trip air ticket from Paris to Casablanca. Later, he
organized a second trip for 300 people, and Nouvelles Frontières was
born. They now have 132 offices worldwide, and some of the cheapest flights to or from the French-speaking world.

Nouvelles Frontières fought the airline cartel in a landmark 1985 case
before the European Court of Justice, and won the right to sell discounted airfares.

FRANKFURT, GERMANY

MARKET TRENDS

Frankfurt Flughafen is the busiest airport in Germany, and the second busiest in Europe. The discount-ticket market is quite competitive, in spite of the government's disdain for consolidator-style discounts. But entrepreneurial spirit dies hard, and the German travel marketplace is no exception. While consolidators as such are well hidden, the market is overflowing with charter offerings. Tour operators (listed in this chapter as discount travel agents) and their charter flights offer your best chance for a budget flight out of Germany. Peruse the ads in the Friday or Saturday *Frankfurter Rundschau* to find additional budget flights. If flying courier strikes your fancy, Frankfurt's bankers produce mounds of documents which need to be somewhere else, fast. Generally speaking, low season is January to March, mid-season is April to August, and high season is September to December.

STOPPING OVER IN FRANKFURT

Once the home office of Hessian mercenary soldiers, Frankfurt is now the financial hub of Germany. Locals refer to it derisively as "Bankfurt," which may not be unfair. But Frankfurt is also the hub of German technomusic and host of a major university, so you will run into black-clad poets just as often as briefcase-clutching number crunchers.

Even the formidable Hessians could not stop the Allies' relentless bombing during World War II. Virtually all of the city's historical buildings were flattened then, and have since been replaced with the skyscrapers of today's metropolis. Of course there are less imposing neighborhoods as well, such as the relaxed and classic **Sachsenhausen**, or the blue collar and alternative **Bockenheim**, which houses an ethnically diverse population as well as the university.

For nightlife reminiscent of New Orleans, check out **Jazzgasse** ("Jazz Alley"), officially known as Kleine Bockenheimer Strasse. Most nights you will find live music here, courtesy of some of Germany's finest jazz players.

If after a few days here you feel the urge to flee, consider getting a

TELEPHONE COUNTRY CODE:
(49)
CURRENCY:
Deutschemark
US$1.00 = 1,50DM

shared ride in a private car. A whole lot safer than hitchhiking, the **Mitfahrzentrale** office [near the Hauptbahnhof at Baseler Str. 7, ☎ (069) 23 64 44] matches riders with cars headed in the right direction. The drivers are usually students, to whom riders pay a token sum per kilometer of the ride.

CHEAP SLEEPS

Haus der Jugend (HI)
Deutschherrnufer 12
Frankfurt, GERMANY
☎ (069) 61 90 58

The best deal in Frankfurt, the Haus is located just a few blocks east of the museums and taverns in Sachsenhausen. Rates in dorm rooms start at DM24, including linen and breakfast. Quads, doubles and singles run progressively higher. The midnight curfew is purely hypothetical, although you can pay a key deposit if you are worried about being locked out. The pleasant patio space is great for meeting fellow travelers.

You are less likely to run into tourists and GI's in the Westend. Near the university and the Palmgarten, try **Pension Backer** at Mendelssohnstr. 92 [☎ (069) 74 79 92]. The location is more than respectable, and convenient to the Westend U-Bahn station. Singles go for DM25-45, doubles for DM65, triples for DM85.

Camping is another option. Just west of Sachsenhausen you will find a site at Niederrader Ufer 20 [☎ (069) 67 38 46]. Take Tram No. 15 from central Sachsenhausen.

CHEAP EATS

For apple wine and food like mom would make (if she were traditional and German), check out **Wagner**, at Schweitzer Str. 17 in Sachsenhausen. The atmosphere is lively, and popular enough that you may have to wait for a table. Nearby **Nachteule** (Schifferstr. 3) is a well-known late-night hangout, with heaping plates pouring out of the kitchen until 4am.

In Bockenheim, when sausage and potatoes are getting you down, try **Ban Thai**. At Leipziger Str. 26, you'll get a nice contrast to the blandness of cabbage, for a decent price to boot.

If budgetary concerns pervade your consciousness, grab a hearty lunch at the **University Mensa**. This is a student cafeteria, so you'll need some remotely believable form of student ID to get the big discounts, like full meals for 4 to 6DM. No ID? You might never even be asked for it, and the regular prices are still reasonable. Located at Bockenheimer Landstr. 120, adjacent to U-Bahn Bockenheimer Warte. Open weekdays from 9am to 4pm.

TO & FROM THE AIRPORT

The national train company, Deutsche Bundesbahn (DB), operates a train from the airport's Bahnhof to the Hauptbahnhof. Trains depart every 15 minutes, and the trip lasts about 11 minutes. The fare is DM3.80, from the ticket machine at the baggage claim in Hall B. The city's FVV also runs two S-Bahn subway lines which connect the airport to the Hauptbahnhof. Interrail and Eurail tickets are valid on both the DB and the S-Bahn trains. From the Hauptbahnhof, you can catch a train to about anywhere in Europe, or catch tram #11 (or walk 15 minutes) to the old city center.

UNIQUELY FRANKFURT

A relaxing alternative to the claustrophobic metropolis is the mostly pedestrianized **Sachsenhausen** district, on the southern bank of the Main River. The "Pedestrians Only" restriction is probably a wise one, since this neighborhood is known as the "apple wine quarter," after the local and wildly popular specialty. The district is also home to the **Museumsufer**, a cluster of seven museums lined up on Schaumainkai. Wander through it as if at a food court, stopping here and there to sample the offerings. Many museums have free admission. On Saturdays, the Museumsufer hosts a large flea market (Flohmarkt), with stalls and museums combining in a wonderful "art and artifacts" motif.

Council Travel

Graf Adolf Strasse 18
Dusseldorf, GERMANY
☎ (0211) 32 90 88
Fax 0211/ 32 04 75

Times to Call: 9am to 5pm
Type of Provider: Discount travel agent
Areas of Specialty: Worldwide

DESTINATIONS	SAMPLE ROUND TRIP FARE	STANDARD ECONOMY FARE
Bangkok	1,190DM	5,845DM
London	285DM	1,047DM
Los Angeles	690DM	6,006DM
New York	499DM	3,872DM

In Business Since: 1947
Payment Methods: Cash, personal check, electronic funds transfer

This office is not actually located in Frankfurt, but books many of its cheapest flights through there, and is reliably cheap enough to merit inclusion. Its best deals are on flights to the USA. One-way tickets available. Additional office in Munich, [☎ (089) 39 50 22].

(See the Council Travel listing in the Chicago chapter for company background.)

Last Minute Borse

Bornheiner Landstrasse 60
Frankfurt/Main GERMANY
☎ (069) 44 00 01
Fax 069/ 597 0733

Times to Call: 9am to 5pm
(Lengthy informational recording in German available after hours.)
Type of Provider: Discount travel agent
Areas of Specialty: Worldwide

DESTINATIONS	SAMPLE ROUND TRIP FARE	STANDARD ECONOMY FARE
Athens	610DM	2,472DM
Bangkok	1,239DM	5,845DM

Djakarta	1,489DM	6,662DM
London	285DM	1,047DM
Los Angeles	999DM	6,006DM
Madrid	569DM	1,872DM
New York	529DM	3,872DM
Sydney	1,769DM	7,703DM
Tokyo	1,929DM	8,190DM

Payment Methods: Cash, money order, certified check, personal
check, Visa, MasterCard, American Express
In Business Since: 1987

Linehaul Express

Flughafen Franchtzentrum, Geb. 453, Zl. 5053
60549 Frankfurt/Main GERMANY
☎ (069) 69 79 32 60
Fax 069/ 69 79 32 62

Times to Call: 9am to 5pm
Type of Provider: Courier company
Areas of Specialty: Asia and Australia

DESTINATIONS	SAMPLE ROUND TRIP FARE	STANDARD ECONOMY FARE	LENGTH OF STAY
Bangkok	1,600DM	5,845DM	Up to 3 mos.
Hong Kong	1,100DM	6,792DM	Up to 3 mos.
Manila	1,300DM	6,859DM	Up to 3 mos.
Singapore	1,600DM	5,942DM	Up to 3 mos.
Sydney	1,200DM	7,703DM	Up to 3 mos.
Taipei	1,300DM	7,023DM	Up to 3 mos.
Tokyo	1,550DM	8,190DM	Up to 3 mos.

Payment Methods: Cash, certified check, personal check, or bank
transfer
Courier Duties on Return Trip: Yes
Minimum Age: 18 years
In Business Since: 1989
Recommended Advance Reservations: 6 to 8 weeks

Contact Peter Fischer, Sylvia Poidinger, or Robert Hagelberger to book
a flight. A 50 percent down payment is required at the time of book-

ing, with the remainder due 30 days before departure.

Flights to Bangkok, Manila, Singapore, Taipei, and Tokyo require a stopover in Hong Kong. The Sydney flight can be arranged with a stopover in Hong Kong, if you prefer. One-way flights are available on some sectors.

Because Linehaul Express is the general sales agent for Cathay Pacific Wholesale Courier, all flights are on Cathay Pacific Airlines. Linehaul can book excursion tickets in conjunction with their long haul flights to many destinations in the Far East to which courier flights are not available. Additional Linehaul Express offices in London and Hong Kong.

Saeed Flugreisen

Mainzer Lanstrasse 71-3
Frankfurt/Main GERMANY
☎ (069) 23 19 72
Fax 069/ 23 42 99

Times to Call: 9am to 5pm
Type of Provider: Discount travel agent
Areas of Specialty: Worldwide

DESTINATIONS	SAMPLE ROUND TRIP FARE	STANDARD ECONOMY FARE
Athens	630DM	2,472DM
Bangkok	1,239DM	5,845DM
London	295DM	1,047DM
Los Angeles	999DM	6,006DM
Madrid	579DM	1,872DM
New York	579DM	3,872DM
Sydney	1,769DM	7,703DM
Tokyo	1,969DM	8,190DM

Payment Methods: Cash, money order, certified check, personal check, Visa, MasterCard, American Express
In Business Since: 1988

SRID Reisen

Berger Strasse 118

60316 Frankfurt/Main GERMANY

☎ (069) 43 01 91

Fax 069/ 43 98 58

Times to Call: 10am to 6pm

Type of Provider: Discount travel agency

Areas of Specialty: Worldwide

DESTINATIONS	SAMPLE ROUND TRIP FARE	STANDARD ECONOMY FARE
Athens	610DM	2,472DM
Bangkok	1,239DM	5,845DM
Djakarta	1,489DM	6,662DM
London	285DM	1,047DM
Los Angeles	999DM	6,006DM
Madrid	569DM	1,872DM
New York	529DM	3,872DM
Sydney	1,769DM	7,703DM
Tokyo	1,929DM	8,190DM

Payment Methods: Cash, bank transfer

In Business Since: 1975

Member of the STA Travel Network. STA is the world's largest travel organization for students and young, independent travelers. They have 120 locations worldwide. Some of their best fares require student ID, or carry a maximum age.

Their tickets are highly flexible, usually good for one year and requiring no advance purchase. Date changes can be made at any office worldwide for $25; refunds cost only $50 to $75. Such flexible tickets are a wise choice for travelers going on long trips without fully concrete itineraries. STA tickets are priced based on one-way tickets, which makes it easy to book open-jaw flights.

LONDON, ENGLAND

CHAPTER 11

MARKET TRENDS

The Mecca of budget travelers worldwide, London has it all. Penny-pinching pilgrims will find more charter flights and courier runs here than anywhere in the world. What's more, London is the birthplace of the bucket shop, a form of business which first showed up here a quarter of a century ago. You will find cheap flights to everywhere in the world, including such pricy destinations as Africa and South America. Check the weeklies (see Uniquely London, below) for the latest discount travel advertisements, or pick up a copy of the *Evening Standard*. As in San Francisco, some London bucket shops can sell tickets by mail to travelers outside Britain, for travel between cities just about anywhere in the world.

Citizens of most of Asia, Africa, Eastern Europe, and Latin America need both visas and onward tickets in order to enter the country.

STOPPING OVER IN LONDON

London is immense, but it sprawls with a certain staid dignity which escapes the average metropolis. The classic architecture and scenic Thames make it a sight to see, while its varied, never-ending activity makes it enjoyable to visit.

Big Ben, red double-decker buses, and the ubiquitous fish-and-chip stands satisfy most preconceptions of London. But underlying all that is an infinite web of interesting subcultures and lively activity which would take more than one lifetime to explore thoroughly. Inside the ancient Roman walls of the one-square-mile **City of London** lies the banking hub of modern Europe. Just outside the walls is the **East End**, a down-and-dirty neighborhood now known as much for its artist colonies as for its role as home to Jack the Ripper. During the **Notting Hill Carnival** (early August), you will see more samba lines than sipping of tea, as the local West Indian community gives Rio de Janeiro some real competition.

Admit from the outstart that you simply cannot see it all, then make some educated decisions about where to spend your time. First-time visitors can orient themselves by taking a quick bus tour of London's

> **TELEPHONE COUNTRY CODE:**
>
> ## (44)
>
> **CURRENCY:**
> Pound Sterling
> US$1.00 = £0.62

famous sights and districts. **The Original London Transport Sightseeing Tour** whisks you through most of London in an open-top double-decker bus. The trip lasts 90 minutes. The £12 price is a better deal if you buy it after noon, because you can then use it to hop on and off the circuit all day, both the day of purchase and the next. Wait for a live guide, found on every other bus.

Don't miss the boat trip down the **River Thames**. Ferries run every 20 minutes from Westminster Bridge to the Tower of London. The trip lasts 30 minutes, costs £3, and is a pleasant place to have a picnic lunch. Even better, continue under Tower Bridge all the way out to **Greenwich**, taking in some of the most spectacular views in London. Return to central London on the nifty, new trains of the Docklands Light Railway.

The **London Underground**, alias "the tube," makes it easy to move between the various neighborhoods of London. If you are staying for more than 3 days, get a weekly pass. Avoid the expensive London Visitor Travel Card, which at £33 no Londoner would dream of buying. Instead, get a one-week Zone 1 Travelcard for £12. On the rare occasion that you need to venture outside Zone 1, you pay a small add-on fare. You'll need a passport-style photo, which when transformed into a London Transport ID card, makes for a good souvenir.

At **Hyde Park Speakers' Corner** on Sundays (Tube: Marble Arch) you can listen to some very polished political satirists, although you will have to find them amidst the religious zealots and the crazies. If you find yourself so inspired, you can speak, too.

Nobody knows exactly how many museums there are in London, but two not to be missed are the **Tate Gallery** (for Impressionist and Modernist works), and the **Museum of London** (the key to understanding London from prehistoric times to today.)

Pubs, short for public houses, are neighborhood places where people go to talk (and drink). The farther you go from the touristy neighborhoods, the more likely that you can strike up a conversation with the locals. If people start buying rounds, get your turn in early, before the group gets too big.

London has as broad and diverse a theater scene as New York, and the tickets here are cheaper. In fact, high-altitude student seats for the **Royal Shakespeare Company** can be bought from their box office for just £1! Of course, you will have to sneak down into better seats at intermission. Other theatrical offerings, ranging from musicals to sex comedies, also offer student and standing-room discounts. The afternoon of the show, tickets for some performances are on sale at the half-price booth on Leicester Square. Other forms of nightlife can be a bit pricy in London. One good choice for live bands and modern rock is **The Borderline** (on Trafalgar Square) where the cover rarely exceeds £5.

Of course, a visit to London only is a ridiculously one-sided way to see Britain. For glorious contrast, try to arrange a brief escape to the countryside. One delightful choice is the mountainous **Lake District.** Hike through the fells, picnicking your way from village to village. A bus to **Keswick** is all you really need; from there, friendly locals make hitch-hiking easy (although, our lawyers point out, this is specifically risky and not recommended). Energetic "peak baggers" can hike to their hearts' content. Consider staying on a working sheep ranch! Margaret Harryman and her family run a cozy, traditional English bed and breakfast from their ranch house. Her young sons are quite knowledgeable about sheep, and will gleefully take you on a tour of the whole operation. Great breakfasts, and hostel-level prices [**Keskadale Farm**: Newlands Valley, Keswick, Cumbria CA12 5TS England, ☎ (07687) 78544]. Insider's Tip: go in lambing season, which starts in March.

CHEAP SLEEPS

Oxford Street Youth Hostel (HI)
14-18 Noel Street
London W1 ENGLAND
☎ (071) 734 1618

The happening, central location of this place means it fills up fast. Either book way ahead of time by mail, or call a few days in advance to try to reserve a spot. The famous Soho club scene surrounds you, and conveniently there is no curfew here. Dorm beds in doubles through quads run £18 for non-members, £15 for members. Tube: Oxford Circus.

Dean Court Hotel

57 Inverness Terrace
London W2 ENGLAND
☎ (071) 229 2961
Fax 071/ 727 1190

More of a guest house than a hotel, this place is popular with the young "world traveler" set. Aussies and others take advantage of the weekly and monthly discounts to stay and work in London for a while. The neighborhood is working class, but very close to Kensington Gardens and Hyde Park, and to the Bayswater and Queensway tube stops. Dorm beds in a quad run £14, doubles are £35. The downstairs lounge is a good place to meet other travelers. Breakfast is included, and you can use the kitchen the rest of the day.

Woodville House

107 Ebury Street, Belgravia
London SW1W 9QU ENGLAND
☎ (071) 730 1048
Fax 071/ 730 2574

A classic bed and breakfast, Woodville has small, pleasantly appointed rooms and is conveniently located near Victoria Station. Hostess Rachel Joplin and her husband Ian are the reason this place is a real find. Rachel knows everything there is to know about London, and will help put you on the right track. Looking for a particular restaurant by name? Or is it that you need a little help in choosing that hopelessly romantic spot? Ask Rachel. She can even tell you how to get there by public transit. Ask, too, about Sue Ryder—the Harrods of charity shops. Singles are £36, doubles run about £56, and bunk rooms go for £18 to £25 per person. Nearby, you can lose yourself in the lush gardens surrounding Buckingham Palace.

CHEAP EATS

The meat stalls at **Old Spitalfields Market**, formerly a huge cattle emporium in the rough-edged East End, have been taken over by artists and crafts vendors. The center of the market houses a bizarre fairy tale-inspired sculpture installation, in which trains, musical fountains, and electric-powered humanoids perambulate every 15 minutes. Also in the center is a stage where post-avantgarde fashions are shown, and a pair of indoor athletic fields. Why all this in the Cheap Eats section? Because half a dozen exotic food stalls make their homes in the middle of all this, and you can eat lunch for a couple of pounds. A very genuine tapas restaurant has been plucked straight out of Madrid and dropped down here, too. Take the tube to Liverpool Street station, cross Bishopsgate, and continue two blocks northeast on Brushfield Street.

For a basic English meal, try the **Chelsea Kitchen** (98 Kings Road, SW3), or sister restaurant **The Stockpot** (50 James Street, W1). Both places live up to their motto, "Good meals at prices you can afford." Expect to eat well for under £5 per person. To spice things up a little, head over to the **Great India Restaurant**, at 79 Lower Sloane Street.

TO & FROM THE AIRPORT

From London Heathrow: Ah, direct service to the airport on the city subway system. Other cities (including San Francisco) could learn from London. The Tube's Picadilly Line runs every 5 to 10 minutes from Heathrow through the heart of the city (50 minutes). The fare is £2.80, and you can get to just about anywhere in London with no more than one transfer.

From London Gatwick: Catch British Rail's Gatwick Express, which runs every 15 minutes from the South Terminal to Victoria Station for £8.60, or £6 Second Class. By bus, catch the Flightline No. 777 from North or South Terminals to Victoria Coach Station (70 minutes), with hourly departures for £6.50.

From London Stansted: British Rail's Stansted Express runs twice hourly to London's Liverpool Street Station (30 minutes) for £9.80. By bus, catch the hourly National Express (No. 102, or 097, 098 or 099) to Victoria Coach Station (80 minutes) for £6.

UNIQUELY LONDON

Whatever your fancy, London probably has a club (or two) dedicated exclusively to bringing together people with a shared interest in doing it. The single best way to get off the beaten track in London is to find a group with which you share an interest, and get involved with them. Group meetings are usually free, and usually open to the public. For fairly mainstream groups, as well as weekly concerts and such, pick up one of the London weeklies, such as *Time Out*, *TNT*, and *What's On*. For intellectual pursuits, check out the bulletin boards in the buildings of the University of London's central campus (Tube: Russell Square).

Feel like just hanging out? On weekends, British youth descend upon **Camden Market**, the hippest of the outdoor bazaars, to do exactly that. Just off the historic waterways of Camden Lock, near the Camden Town tube station, this is a great place to peruse used clothing, books and records. By day, grab a table at a café and watch the people, or cruise the stalls and strike up a conversation. By night, you'll find a lively bar scene, and clubs offering everything from jazz bands to the latest house music.

Afro-Asian Travel

162/168 Regent Street, Suite 233
London W1R 5TB ENGLAND
☎ (071) 437 8255
Fax 071/ 437 8250

Times to Call: 9:30am to 5:30pm
Type of Provider: Consolidator
Areas of Specialty: Africa, Asia, India

DESTINATIONS	SAMPLE ROUND TRIP FARE	STANDARD ECONOMY FARE
Bangkok	£330	£2,118
Bombay	£385	£995
Cairo	£265	£934
Johannesburg	£500	£1,046
Los Angeles	£340	£958
Nairobi	£440	£898
Sydney	£680	£1,315
Tel Aviv	£250	£924

Payment Methods: Cash, money order, certified check, personal
check, Visa, MasterCard, Access, American Express
In Business Since: 1971

This company prides itself on its focus on personal service. There is a
small surcharge for credit card purchases. The owner started out selling charter flights from London to Kenya, and gradually shifted into
consolidated tickets.

Bluewheel Travel Ltd.

417 Hendon Way
London NW4 3LH ENGLAND
☎ (081) 202 0111
Fax 081/ 202 3839

Times to Call: 9am to 5pm
Type of Provider: Consolidator
Areas of Specialty: Europe

DESTINATIONS	SAMPLE ROUND TRIP FARE	STANDARD ECONOMY FARE
Amsterdam	£75	£199

✈ Athens	£99	£543	
Istanbul	£140	£606	
Paris	£69	£180	
✈ Rome	£115	£445	
Tel Aviv	£149	£924	

Payment Methods: Cash, money order, certified check, personal check, Visa, MasterCard, American Express (a small fee is charged for use of American Express)
In Business Since: 1992

Those seeking to buy a ticket from abroad should inquire by fax, in order to save on telephone charges. They will respond by fax in a couple of hours.

Bridges Worldwide
☎ (081) 759 8059, (081) 759 5040
Fax 081/ 759 8069

Times to Call: 9am to 5:30pm
Type of Provider: Courier booking agent
Areas of Specialty: Worldwide

DESTINATIONS	SAMPLE ROUND TRIP FARE	STANDARD ECONOMY FARE	LENGTH OF STAY
Bangkok	£275	£2,118	up to 8 weeks
Boston	£299	£682	up to 8 weeks
Los Angeles	£349	£958	up to 8 weeks
Miami	£295	£958	up to 8 weeks
New York	£200	£806	up to 8 weeks
Tokyo	£475	£1,366	up to 8 weeks

Payment Methods: Cash, certified check, personal check, Visa, MasterCard
Courier Duties on Return Trip: No
Minimum Age: 18 years
In Business Since: 1992
Recommended Advance Reservations: 3 months in high season
Luggage: Couriers are allowed to bring 20 kilograms of checked baggage, as well as their carry-ons

Bridges staff say "definitely" call to check on last-minute discounts.

This company maintains a cancellation phone list. One-way tickets available for 60 percent of the round trip fare. Contact Nina Sidhu to reserve a flight.

Other originating cities include Bangkok, Hong Kong, and soon San Francisco. Bridges is the booking agent for courier flights on Virgin Express runs, so all flights are on Virgin Atlantic.

Campus Travel

52 Grosvenor Gardens
London SW1W OAG ENGLAND
☎ (071) 730 8832
Fax 071/ 730 5739

Times to Call: 9am to 6:30pm weekdays, plus Thursday open until 8pm, 10am to 6:30pm Saturday
Type of Provider: Discount travel agent
Areas of Specialty: Worldwide student and youth fares, including around-the-world

DESTINATIONS	SAMPLE ROUND TRIP FARE	STANDARD ECONOMY FARE
Amsterdam	£130	£199
Bangkok	£734	£2,118
Hong Kong	£900	£1,200
Los Angeles	£598	£958
Mexico City	£588	£956
Paris	£134	£180
Prague	£258	£443
New York	£330	£806
Sydney	£958	£1,315

Payment Methods: Cash, check with check card and 10 clear working days, debit card, traveler's checks in Sterling, Visa, MasterCard, American Express
In Business Since: 1959

This main office is located just across the street from Victoria Station. There are 36 other Campus Travel offices in the university towns across the UK, and about 500 affiliated offices worldwide. Campus Travel also books adventure tours and treks geared towards the student market.

Council Travel

28A Poland Street (off Oxford Circus)

London W1V 3DB ENGLAND

☎ (071) 437 7767 for worldwide information

☎ (071) 287 3337 for European information

Fax 071/ 287 9414

Times to Call: 9am to 6pm Monday through Saturday (9am to 7pm Thursday), 10am to 5pm Sunday

Type of Provider: Discount travel agent

Areas of Specialty: Worldwide student, youth, and budget travel

DESTINATIONS	SAMPLE ROUND TRIP FARE	STANDARD ECONOMY FARE
Amsterdam	£68	£199
Bali	£505	n/a
Bangkok	£345	£2,118
Los Angeles	£302	£958
New York	£233	£806
Paris	£68	£180
Prague	£129	£443
Sydney	£675	£1,315
Tel Aviv	£261	£924

Payment Methods: Cash, money order, personal check, Visa, MasterCard, Access

In Business Since: 1947

Expect prices to drop a bit at the last-minute, as specials come out a few weeks before the date of departure.

(See the Council Travel listing in the Chicago chapter for company background.)

Courier Travel Services, Ltd.

346 Fulham Road
London, SW10 9UH ENGLAND
☎ (071) 351 0300
Fax 071/ 351 0170

Times to Call: 9am to 5:30pm
Type of Provider: Courier booking company
Areas of Specialty: Worldwide

DESTINATIONS	SAMPLE ROUND TRIP FARE	STANDARD ECONOMY FARE	LENGTH OF STAY
Cairo	£150	£934	up to 28 days
Harare	£435	£2,074	up to 28 days
Lusaka	£350	£1,851	7 or 15 days
Port Louis	£499	£2,380	15 days
Nairobi	£399	£898	up to 28 days
Miami	£199	£958	up to 28 days
New York	£179	£806	8 or 15 days
San Francisco	£265	£958	up to 28 days
Hong Kong	£449	£1,200	up to 28 days
Tokyo	£429	£1,366	up to 28 days
Rio de Janeiro	£389	£1,564	up to 28 days

Payment Methods: Cash, money order, certified check, personal
check, Visa, MasterCard, American Express
Courier Duties on Return Trip: Yes
Minimum Age: 18 years
In Business Since: 1989
Recommended Advance Reservations: 6 to 8 weeks
Luggage: 23 kilograms of checked luggage, plus carry-ons

One-way tickets available to Tokyo for £225. Call to check on last-minute discounts, which are extremely cheap. This company maintains a cancellation phone list. All flights are on British Airways. Couriers must complete a registration form before becoming eligible to book flights.

German Travel Service

Bridge House

55-59 High Road

Broxbourne Hartfordshire EN10 7DT ENGLAND

☎ (0992) 45 61 46

Fax 0992/ 44 44 88

Times to Call: 9am to 5:30pm Monday to Saturday

Type of Provider: Consolidator

Areas of Specialty: Germany, Europe

DESTINATIONS	SAMPLE ROUND TRIP FARE	STANDARD ECONOMY FARE
Berlin	£142	£380
Dusseldorf	£92	£294
Frankfurt	£117	£259
Hamburg	£124	£358
Munich	£144	£380
New York	tba	£806
Paris	tba	£180
Rome	tba	£445
Zurich	tba	£328

Payment Methods: Cash, money order, certified check, personal check, Visa, MasterCard, American Express

In business since 1952, when it started as a coach company with a single coach. The company consolidates for Lufthansa and Sabena. Separate groups within the company sell airfare and tours to Paris, Amsterdam, Belgium, Eurodisney, and Switzerland. Now adding air only to Europe and the USA. They have been operating package tours to the Continent for years.

Jupiter Air U.K., Ltd.

Jupiter House, Horton Road

Colnbrook, Slough, SL3 0BB ENGLAND

☎ (075) 368 9989

Fax 075/ 368 1661

Times to Call: 9am to 5pm

Type of Provider: Courier company

Areas of Specialty: Worldwide

DESTINATIONS	SAMPLE ROUND TRIP FARE	STANDARD ECONOMY FARE	LENGTH OF STAY
Bangkok	tba	£2,118	7 to 30 days
Hong Kong	tba	£1,200	7 to 30 days
Manila	tba	£1,328	7 to 30 days
New York	£220	£806	1 or 2 wks +
San Francisco	£350	£958	1 or 2 weeks
Singapore	tba	£1,264	7 to 30 days
Sydney	£450-750	£1,315	7 to 30 days
Taipei	tba	£2,264	7 to 30 days

Payment Methods: Cash, money order, certified check, personal check, Visa, Mastercard

In Business Since: 1988

Courier Duties on Return Trip: Yes

Recommended Advance Reservations: 0 to 3 months

Luggage: 20 kilograms of checked luggage plus carry-on

Hong Kong is Jupiter Air's hub city. Thus it is sometimes possible to reserve a courier flight from Hong Kong to other Asian cities, such as Bangkok or Tokyo. Keep in mind that you must be back in Hong Kong in time for your return flight.

This office is located near Heathrow Airport, west of London. Additional offices in Hong Kong, Los Angeles, New York, San Francisco, Seoul, Sydney, Taipei, and Tokyo. Jupiter strongly favors repeat business. One-way fares are available to all destinations. Last-minute flights can be had for 50 percent off. They also maintain a cancellation phone list.

Linehaul Express, Ltd.

Building 252, Section D
Ely Road, Heathrow Airport
Middlesex TW6 2PR ENGLAND
☎ (081) 759 5969
Fax 081/ 759 5973
Contact: Narinder Bal

Times to Call: 8:30am to 4:30pm

Type of Provider: Courier company

Areas of Specialty: Hong Kong and Australia

DESTINATIONS	SAMPLE ROUND TRIP FARE	STANDARD ECONOMY FARE	LENGTH OF STAY
Hong Kong	£450	£1,200	Up to 3 mos.
Sydney	£499	£1,315	Up to 3 mos.

Deposit: £100
Payment Methods: Cash, check, or Visa
Courier Duties on Return Trip: Yes
Minimum Age: 18 years
In Business Since: 1989
Recommended Advance Reservations: 3 months

These flights are available as departures from either London or Manchester. One-way tickets to Hong Kong are available for a bit more than half the round trip price. Flights to Sydney are round trip only. This company maintains a cancellation phone list.

Linehaul is the general sales agent for Cathay Pacific's courier operation, so all flights are on service-oriented Cathay Pacific Airlines. Additional Line Haul Express offices in Frankfurt and Hong Kong.

Norwood Travel

202 Norwood Road
London SE27 9AU ENGLAND
☎ (081) 674 8214
Fax 081/ 674 2542
Contact: Lee

Times to Call: 9am to 5pm
Type of Provider: Courier booking agent
Areas of Specialty: Worldwide

DESTINATIONS	SAMPLE ROUND TRIP FARE	STANDARD ECONOMY FARE	LENGTH OF STAY
Within Europe:			
Barcelona	£89	£387	1 or 2 weeks
Larnaca	£135	£824	8 to 12 days
Lisbon	£99	£379	5 to 10 days
To North America:			
Boston	£210	£682	1 or 2 weeks
Chicago	£249	£958	1 or 2 weeks
Los Angeles	£249	£958	8 to 22 days

Miami	£239	£958	15 days
Montreal	£199	£700	1 or 2 weeks
New York	£210	£806	1 or 2 weeks
Philadelphia	£210	£864	1 or 2 weeks
Seattle	£249	£1,108	2 weeks
Toronto	£239	£700	1 or 2 weeks
Vancouver	n/a	£1,006	2 weeks
Washington, D.C.		£210	1 or 2 weeks

To Africa, Asia, and the Middle East:

Gaborone	£369	£1,436	22 days
Johannesburg	£419	£1,046	3 weeks
Bangkok	£355	£2,118	15 to 17 days
Hong Kong	£450	£ 1,200	2 or 3 weeks
Kuala Lumpur	£399	£1,264	15 days
Singapore	£375	£1,264	2 or 3 weeks
Tokyo	£479	£1,366	2 or 3 weeks
Abu Dhabi	£299	£1,040	8 to 13 days
Bahrain	£299	£1,008	7 to 12 days
Dubai	£299	£1,040	10 days
Tel Aviv	£189	£924	8, 13, 16 days

Payment Methods: Cash, money order, certified check, personal check, Visa, MasterCard

Courier Duties on Return Trip: Yes

Minimum Age: 18 years

In Business Since: 1989

Recommended Advance Reservations: 1 to 3 months

Call to check on last-minute discounts. This company maintains a cancellation phone list.

Nouvelles Frontières

11 Blenheim Street

London W1Y 9LE ENGLAND

☎ (071) 355 3952, (071) 629 7772

Fax 071/ 491 0684

Times to Call: 9am to 5pm

Type of Provider: Consolidator and charter operator

Areas of Specialty: Worldwide

DESTINATIONS	SAMPLE ROUND TRIP FARE	STANDARD ECONOMY FARE
Agadir	£199	£424
Crete	£135	£610
Nice	£135	£393
Paris	£79	£180
Toulouse	£145	£464

Payment Methods: Cash, money order, certified check, personal check, Visa, MasterCard, American Express
In Business Since: 1967

Discount tickets on Tower Air, American Trans Air, Continental, KLM, American Airlines, and CORSAIR.

Started in 1967 by a French law student who was putting together a trip to Morocco for some friends. The entire trip cost a quarter of the price of a round trip air ticket from Paris to Casablanca. Later, he organized a second trip for 300 people, and Nouvelles Frontières was born. They now have 132 offices worldwide, and some of the cheapest flights to or from the French-speaking world.

Nouvelles Frontières fought the airline cartel in a landmark 1985 case before the European Court of Justice, and won the right to sell discounted airfares.

Polo Express

208 Epsom Square
London Heathrow Airport
Hounslow, Middlesex TW6 2BL ENGLAND
☎ (081) 759 5383
Fax 081/ 759 5697
Contact: Denise

Times to Call: 9am to 4:30pm
Type of Provider: Courier company
Areas of Specialty: Worldwide

DESTINATIONS	SAMPLE ROUND TRIP FARE	STANDARD ECONOMY FARE	LENGTH OF STAY
Within Europe:			
Barcelona	£89	£387	1 or 2 weeks
Larnaca	£135	£824	8 to 12 days
Lisbon	£99	£379	5 to 10 days
To North America:			
Boston	£210	£682	1 or 2 weeks
Chicago	£249	£958	1 or 2 weeks
Los Angeles	£249	£958	8 to 22 days
Miami	£239	£958	15 days
Montreal	£199	£700	1 or 2 weeks
New York	£210	£806	1 or 2 weeks
Philadelphia	£210	£864	1 or 2 weeks
Seattle	£249	£1,108	2 weeks
Toronto	£239	£700	1 or 2 weeks
Vancouver	n/a	£1,006	2 weeks
Washington, D.C.		£210	1 or 2 weeks
To Africa, Asia, and the Middle East:			
Gaborone	£369	£1,436	22 days
Johannesburg	£419	£1,046	3 weeks
Bangkok	£355	£2,118	15 to 17 days
Hong Kong	£450	£ 1,200	2 or 3 weeks
Kuala Lumpur	£399	£1,264	15 days
Singapore	£375	£1,264	2 or 3 weeks
Tokyo	£479	£1,366	2 or 3 weeks
Abu Dhabi	£299	£1,040	8 to 13 days
Bahrain	£299	£1,008	7 to 12 days
Dubai	£299	£1,040	10 days
Tel Aviv	£169	£924	8 to 16 days

Payment Methods: Cash, money order, certified check, Visa, MasterCard

Courier Duties on Return Trip: Yes

Minimum Age: 18 years

In Business Since: 1989

Recommended Advance Reservations: 2 to 3 months

Luggage: One checked bag (max. 44 lbs / 23 kgs) and one carry-on

Last minute discounts galore! Polo is an official groundhandler for British Airways cargo service, so all flights from London are on British

Airways. Rates are about 40 percent lower in the off-season, and especially low in January.

STA Travel

117 Euston Road
London NW1 2SX ENGLAND
☎ (071) 938 4711
Fax 071/ 938 5321

Times to Call: 9am to 5pm
Type of Provider: Discount travel agency
Areas of Specialty: Worldwide

DESTINATIONS	SAMPLE ROUND TRIP FARE	STANDARD ECONOMY FARE
Amsterdam	£69	£199
Bangkok	£379	£2,118
Ho Chi Minh City	£499	n/a
Los Angeles	£239	£958
Madrid	£84	£413
Mexico City	£286	£956
New York	£156	£806
Paris	£69	£180
Rio de Janeiro	£399	£1,564
Sydney	£622	£1,315

Payment Methods: Cash, money order, certified check, personal check, Visa, MasterCard, American Express
In Business Since: 1975

STA is the world's largest travel organization for students and young, independent travelers. They have 120 locations worldwide. Some of their best fares require student ID, or carry a maximum age.

Their tickets are highly flexible, usually good for one year and requiring no advance purchase. Date changes can be made at any office worldwide for $25; refunds cost only $50 to $75. Such flexible tickets are a wise choice for travelers going on long trips without fully concrete itineraries. STA tickets are priced based on one-way tickets, which makes it easy to book open-jaw flights.

Trailfinders

194 Kensington High Street
London W8 7RG ENGLAND
☎ (071) 938 3232, for flights within Europe
☎ (071) 938 3939, for flights elsewhere
Fax 071/ 938 3305

Times to Call: 9am to 6pm Monday through Saturday (9am to 7pm
Thursday), 10am to 4pm Sunday
Type of Provider: Consolidator
Areas of Specialty: Worldwide

DESTINATIONS	SAMPLE ROUND TRIP FARE	STANDARD ECONOMY FARE
Bangkok	£379	£2,118
Los Angeles	£306	£958
Paris	£83	£180
New York	£195	£806
Sydney	£597	£1,315
Tel Aviv	£239	£924

Payment Methods: Cash, money order, certified check, personal
check, Visa, MasterCard, American Express
In Business Since: 1970

Trailfinders asks us to point out that they are unable to sell discounted fares for travel commencing outside the UK. In practice, this
means that people starting from the Continent, for example, need to
fly to London, and then start their discount itinerary from there. This
is in fact a common occurrence, and can result in very substantial savings. These conditions are imposed by the airlines, and Trailfinders
does enforce them strictly.

Trailfinders is one of the most well-known and well-respected consolidators in the world. They have added a "one-stop travel shop"
which includes an immunization center, visa service, American
Express traveler's checks, book shop, and a reference library.

USA Travel Centre, Ltd.

8 Hogarth Road
Earls Court
London SW5 0PT ENGLAND
☎ (071) 373 8383, (071) 835 1189
Fax 071/ 373 3323

Times to Call: 9am to 5pm
Type of Provider: Charter operator
Areas of Specialty: USA

DESTINATIONS	SAMPLE ROUND TRIP FARE	STANDARD ECONOMY FARE
Athens	£139	£543
Los Angeles	£269	£958
Miami	£299	£958
New York	£199	£806
Orlando	£199	£958
Rome	£139	£445

Payment Methods: Cash, certified check, personal check, Visa,
MasterCard, American Express
In Business Since: 1991

Works with tourist bureaus in each of the 50 states to promote British tourism in the USA. Also books a lot of flights for Americans traveling from London to the continent. The USA Travel Centre books flights on major carriers such as Virgin Air, as well as charter companies such as American Trans Air.

Worldwide Cheap Travel Service

First Floor, 254 Earls Court Road
London SW5 9AD ENGLAND
☎ (071) 373 6465
Fax 071/ 370 3425

Times to Call: 10am to 6:30pm Monday to Friday, 10am to 5pm
Saturday
Type of Provider: Consolidator
Areas of Specialty: Worldwide

DESTINATIONS	SAMPLE ROUND TRIP FARE	STANDARD ECONOMY FARE
Bangkok	£320	£2,118
Los Angeles	£299	£958
Paris	£69	£180
Sydney	£599	£1,315
Tel Aviv	£169	£924

Payment Methods: Cash, money order, certified check, personal check, Visa, MasterCard, American Express

In Business Since: 1981

WCTS specializes in cheap flights to Europe and the Far East. They can also get you deals on Business and First-Class flights to and from the USA.

BANGKOK, THAILAND

MARKET TRENDS

Thailand teems with budget airfare opportunities, but some caution is advised. Consolidators congregate near the guest houses on Khao San Road, and near the Malaysia Hotel. Convincing but fake passports, drivers licenses (said to be crucial for those under 21 years of age and headed for the USA) and student IDs can be purchased in the same neighborhoods. Avoid J Travel—people have complained about them for decades. Keep an ear to the street. You will hear the latest news about companies who sell tickets on planes that do not exist. Luckily, credit cards are widely accepted.

Many travelers consider Bangkok the gateway to Burma, Cambodia, and Vietnam. This can be true, but for a quick trip, many U.S. and British consolidators can get you a better deal if you book straight through to your final destination (with an optional stopover in Bangkok, but all on one ticket). Local travel agents can usually arrange visas for you, for a small fee.

Courier flights from Bangkok can be fantastic deals for those taking quick trips. On occasion, companies will sell (and even give away) one-way courier flights at the last-minute, so it can be worthwhile to call and ask.

Thai customs officials will accept "sufficient funds" as proof that you can support yourself in the country. No onward ticket is required, just show them that you have enough cash in your moneybelt.

STOPPING OVER IN BANGKOK

Bangkok can seem overwhelming at first. Visitors are greeted by a cacophony of blaring motorscooter horns, roaring tuk tuks, singsonging vendors, and glittering temples, all shrouded at times by the faint, sweet scent of rotting vegetation or the acrid tang of car exhaust.

The sheer number of wats, or Buddhist temples, can also be overwhelming. There are almost 400 of these traditional sites in Bangkok alone. One of the most famous is **Wat Po**, home of the reclining Buddha, which is located along the Chaophrya River just south of the

TELEPHONE COUNTRY CODE:
(66)
CURRENCY:
Baht
US$1.00 = 25B

151

Grand Palace and on the southern fringe of Banglampoo. It is also peaceful to wander through the beautifully landscaped grounds of some of the smaller neighborhood wats.

Massage in Thailand has lots of sexual overtones, but on the temple grounds at Wat Po, you can get a non-sexual, traditional Thai massage for a moderate fee. The tables are outside, in the open air, and the massages are given by students working to earn their licenses.

The **Grand Palace** and **Temple of the Emerald Buddha** are crowded with tourists, but still important to visit. Bear in mind the dress code: no leather shoes, no shorts, and no sleeveless shirts. You can always rent appropriate apparel from vendors outside the site.

A note on prostitution. Admittedly, it happens in all parts of the world. What makes the Asian sex trade different is that some prostitutes are literally girls, usually 12 to 14 years old, sometimes younger. They are not consenting adults, and are not typically in this trade by choice. More likely they have been drugged, kidnapped, or even sold by their own parents into the brothels. They will almost assuredly die of AIDS by age 25. Consider the implications carefully before you support this wretched business.

The feel you get for Bangkok can depend on the weather while you are there. In the really hot, dry times, people can seem worn out and are less likely to make the effort to be friendly. So a visit during dusty, hot, and polluted April will be a whole lot different that a trip during cool and relaxing December. Rains are heaviest from June to November.

River sightseeing tip: take the public river taxis instead of hiring your own boat. When you share a "long-tailed taxi" (rua hang yao) with the locals, you get to experience dogs and babies coming out to the dock's end to greet whomever is coming home. The rua hang yao (10B) go up the same side canals for a whole lot less than the private boat tours (750B), and they are infinitely more social and entertaining. The private boat operators may tell you that the public taxis don't exist—don't believe a word of it. Stay by the pier and watch what happens. And pay the public taxi operator only what everyone else is paying—as a farang (foreigner), you can be seen as an easy mark. If the taxi stops for lunch somewhere, be flexible, and take the opportunity to do some off-the-beaten-track exploring.

If you must attempt to forge the gridlocked streets, there is rarely a need to splurge on a land-based taxi. The extensive bus network is crowded, but very cheap. Fares are under 5B. Pick up a copy of Bangkok's best map, appropriately titled *No. 1 Best Seller*. This yellow, green, and red map identifies all sights in both English and Thai script, making it easy for any passerby to locate your destination. It also shows the bus routes.

Bangkok can be crowded and oppressive, so if you can stay for more than a few days, consider taking the three hour train ride from Thonburi Station to **Kanchanaburi**. This laid-back small city is very popular with Thai tourists, due largely to its scenic location, which was portrayed in the movie *Bridge over the River Kwai*. Stay in a riverside bungalow for 10B a night. **Rick's Lodge** is a good choice, since they have a great restaurant and speak perfect English.

CHEAP SLEEPS

Try to stay in places near the river, because travel by river is much more pleasant than travel in a steamy, gridlock-bound taxi. You'll find the three- and four-star hotels in the **Sukumvit** and **Siam** districts, but they are a bit far from the markets, temples, clubs, and backpackers in the Banglampoo area. Khau San Road is the best-known street in **Banglampoo**, so the two terms are roughly synonymous. Keep in mind that taxi drivers get a commission for bringing guests to certain guest houses, so be insistent if they tell you that the place you wanted to go to has burned down, closed for health reasons, etc.

The high season for tourism is January and February, during which time it is wise to reserve rooms in advance, or at least start looking early in the morning, before the best places are taken.

Bangkok Youth Hostel (HI)
25/2 Phitsanulok Road
Sisao Theves, Dusit
Bangkok 10300 THAILAND
☎ (02) 281 0361, (02) 282 0950
Fax 02/ 281 6834

The hostel is a ten-minute walk north of Banglampoo, near the river and National Museum, and in a much quieter neighborhood than the Khao San Road guest houses. Dorm beds go for 50B a night, while rooms range from 80–160B. There are dozens of guest houses in this area as well.

My House

37 Soi Chanasongkhram
Phra Athit Road
Bangkok 10200 THAILAND
☎ (02) 282 9263, (02) 282 9264

50-100B per night, ultra-basic accommodations near the river in Banglampoo.

New Siam Guest House

21 Soi Chanasongkhram, Phra Athit
Bangkok 10200 THAILAND

Right off of Phra Athit, on an alley near the main express-river-taxi stop. Rooms go for about 350B a night, including air-conditioning, shower curtains and similar amenities that are rare for this price. Lockers, good breakfasts, and a travel agency downstairs. Young crowd. Good English is spoken by the wonderfully helpful manager. This place tends to be full, so you may have to reserve a room for tomorrow, and stay the first night at any nearby guest house.

CHEAP EATS

There seems to be more food for sale in Bangkok than anywhere else in the world. It is as if the Thais never eat at home. You will find lots of good, cheap eateries.

Food stalls are a classic bargain food option, and an opportunity to eat with the locals. The stalls on **Phra Athit Road** in Banglampoo are no exception. A bit further south, a great deal for lunch awaits at **Thammasat University's** outdoor dining hall, where rice dishes go for 10B.

You will find authentic, high quality Thai food for a fair price at **Wang Nar**, on the riverbank under the Phra Pinklao Bridge. Outdoor deck and air-conditioned seating are available.

Because of the language barrier, many travelers end up eating their meals at the guest houses. This strategy results in plain but easy dining. Try the food stalls for variety.

TO & FROM THE AIRPORT

By bus, walk out of the airport building and turn left to find the bus stop. Air-conditioned buses No. 4, 10, or 13 will take you into the city for 20B. Beware, chaos ensues on these buses during rush hour. Unfortunately, most flights from the USA arrive in Bangkok after 10pm, when the buses have stopped. At that time of night, your best bet is to share a cab with people you have met on the plane. Just outside customs you will spot a taxi stand, with cabs to Banglampoo running about 230B. Every guest house sells 50B tickets for the shuttle back to the airport.

UNIQUELY BANGKOK

The **Talaat Tehweht Public Flower Market**, awash in the aroma of blooming orchids, is a great place for an evening stroll. Start at the Grand Palace or at Wat Po anytime after 4pm, and wander south along the river until you find yourself in the midst of the market, which runs along the mouth of the Klong Krung Kasem canal. Huge bouquets go for about 25B.

Bridges Worldwide

Air Cargo Bay
Bangkok International Airport
Bangkok, THAILAND
☎ (02) 533 4066
Fax 02/ 533 6179
Contact: Nipa

Times to Call: 9:30am to 5:30pm
Type of Provider: Courier company
Areas of Specialty: Asia

DESTINATIONS	SAMPLE ROUND TRIP FARE	STANDARD ECONOMY FARE	LENGTH OF STAY
Hong Kong	4,500B	6,405B	up to one year
Singapore	2,300B	6,100B	up to 14 days

Payment Methods: Cash, money order, certified check, personal
check
Minimum Age: 18 years
In Business Since: 1989
Recommended Advance Reservations: 2 weeks

One-way tickets available to Hong Kong and Singapore.
Call to check on last-minute discounts and free flights!

Jupiter Air (Siam Trans International)

78 Kiatnakin Building
Bushlane, New Road
Bangkok 10500 THAILAND
☎ (02) 235 6741, (02) 235 6751
Fax 02/ 236 1042
Contact: Sirirat

Times to Call: 10am to 7pm
Type of Provider: Courier company
Areas of Specialty: Worldwide

DESTINATIONS	SAMPLE ROUND TRIP FARE	STANDARD ECONOMY FARE	LENGTH OF STAY
Hong Kong	4000B	6,405B	14 days
Los Angeles	18,000B	48,590B	1 month
San Francisco	18,000B	48,590B	1 month

156

Singapore	4000B	6,100B	14 days	*Bangkok*

Payment Methods: Cash or check
In Business Since: 1988
Recommended Advance Reservations: 2 weeks
Courier duties: Both to and from destination

The San Francisco and Los Angeles flights are not very regular, so call to check on the schedule.

Hong Kong is Jupiter Air's hub city. Thus it is sometimes possible to reserve a courier flight from Hong Kong to other Asian cities, such as Bangkok or Tokyo. Keep in mind that you must be back in Hong Kong in time for your return flight.

Additional offices in Hong Kong, Los Angeles, New York, San Francisco, Seoul, Sydney, Taipei, and Tokyo. Jupiter strongly favors repeat business.

Oscar Tours

74-10 Petchburi Road, Suite 31
Bangkok 10400 THAILAND
☎ (02) 254 4515
Fax 02/ 253 7536
Contact: Rachanee

Times to Call: 9am to 5pm Monday to Saturday
Type of Provider: Consolidator
Areas of Specialty: Middle East and Europe

DESTINATIONS	SAMPLE ROUND TRIP FARE	STANDARD ECONOMY FARE
Dubai	call	32,860B
Frankfurt	call	62,200B
London	call	65,995B
Rome	call	58,520B
Zurich	call	61,480B

Payment Methods: Cash, money order, certified check, personal check, Visa, MasterCard, American Express
In Business Since: 1991

Flights on Thai International to Dubai, connecting to Emirates Air flights to Europe. Their contract with the airlines does not allow them to print their prices, but the fares they quote over the telephone or in person will amaze you.

STA Travel

Thai Hotel
78 Prachatipatai Road
Visutikasat, Bangkok 10200 THAILAND
☎ (02) 281 5314, (02) 281 5315
Fax 02/ 280 1388

Times to Call: 8:30am to 5pm
Type of Provider: Discount travel agency
Areas of Specialty: Worldwide

DESTINATIONS	SAMPLE ROUND TRIP FARE	STANDARD ECONOMY FARE
London	25,500B	65,995B
Los Angeles	21,000B	48,590B
New York	25,400B	84,910B
Paris	23,500B	62,200B
Sydney	15,000B	48,450B

Payment Methods: Cash, money order, certified check, personal check, Visa, MasterCard, American Express
In Business Since: 1975

STA is the world's largest travel organization for students and young, independent travelers. They have 120 locations worldwide. Some of their best fares require student ID, or carry a maximum age.

Their tickets are highly flexible, usually good for one year and requiring no advance purchase. Date changes can be made at any office worldwide for $25; refunds cost only $50 to $75. Such flexible tickets are a wise choice for travelers going on long trips without fully concrete itineraries. STA tickets are priced based on one-way tickets, which makes it easy to book open-jaw flights.

Vista Travel Service

24/4 Khao San Road
Banglampoo, Bangkok
☎ (02) 280 0348
Fax 02/ 281 5579

Times to Call: 9am to 5pm
Type of Provider: Consolidator
Areas of Specialty: Worldwide

DESTINATIONS	SAMPLE ROUND TRIP FARE	STANDARD ECONOMY FARE
London	19,100B	65,995B
Los Angeles	20,700B	48,590B
New York	29,200B	84,910B
Sydney	14,900B	48,450B

Payment Methods: Cash, money order, certified check, personal
check, Visa, MasterCard, American Express
In Business Since: 1984

There is a surcharge for credit card transactions.

HONG KONG

CHAPTER 13

MARKET TRENDS

Hong Kong is one of Asia's most popular tourist destinations. During vacation periods, including Christmas, summer, and especially Chinese New Year, all but the most expensive airline seats are nearly impossible to come by. Try to book your flight two to three months in advance if you plan to travel at these busy times. The Hong Kong market has caught on to the amazing deals available to couriers, most commonly on flights within Asia. You should call on the first day of the month in order to book a courier flight two to three months later.

To get a feel for the market, look for ads in the *South China Morning Post*. But beware, there are very occasional reports of bait-and-switch schemes, if not outright fraud, encountered by people doing business with Hong Kong consolidators. Use credit cards when possible, and pay only upon receipt of a confirmed ticket (call the airline first) when plastic is not accepted. Customs officials will usually accept "sufficient funds" in lieu of the onward tickets normally required to enter the country. Guest houses and hostels, while occasionally a bit grimy, are for the most part plentiful and tolerable.

STOPPING OVER IN HONG KONG

The "Pearl of the Orient," as Hong Kong is often called, is indeed a wondrous place to visit. From the time one enters Hong Kong airspace and endures the crazy, wide-eyed landing over Kowloon Tong, there is an adventure around every turn.

Hong Kong—which means "fragrant harbor" in Cantonese—is a city of endless contrasts. Just a ten minute ride or a brisk hour's walk straight uphill from one of the world's most active financial centers, a traveler can easily get lost in reverie on **Victoria Peak** (simply "The Peak" to locals). It's a must for any traveler, especially at night. (Take the Peak Tram from Garden Road on Hong Kong Island. There is a free shuttle from the Star Ferry Terminal. The tram ride takes about 10 minutes each way and costs about HK$20 each for a round trip ticket).

Note: no city codes are required for calls within Hong Kong. Also, Hong Kong telephone numbers will change on January 1, 1995. All numbers will be prefixed with the digit 2, to become 8 digits long.

TELEPHONE COUNTRY CODE:

(852)

CURRENCY:
Hong Kong Dollar
US$1.00 = HK$7.10

Public transportation is generally fast and easy. Buses, trams and the subway (called the Mass Transit Railway, or MTR) have frequent stops through the territory and are inexpensive. Be sure to carry a lot of change, though; in most cases exact change is required. Another tip for getting around involves the lobby of the **Kowloon Hotel**, where there is a computer which will print out in Chinese characters the name of the sights you hope to visit on a given day. Sure, the machine probably exists for hotel guests to use, but it is self-service, and it sure makes asking for directions easier.

Of course, the big question on the minds of all Hong Kong-bound tourists (and for that matter, Hong Kong residents) is what will happen when the British relinquish control in 1997. Changes have already begun, but there's still time to catch Hong Kong in its glory. The Hong Kong economy continues to grow by leaps and bounds, and if China follows up on its pledge of relative non-intervention, this growth will likely continue for years to come.

The green ferries of the Star Line shuttle back and forth between **Kowloon** and **Hong Kong Island**. For the cost of a cheap cup of coffee, you get a close-up of one of the most dramatic harbor cityscapes in the world. At the same time, the harbor itself is a chaotic whirlpool of cargo carriers, British warships, cruise liners, fishing sampans, junks and oar-driven dragon boats. By the time you arrive there the British may be gone, but the sampans will remain.

CHEAP SLEEPS

Lodgings in Hong Kong range from cheap and seedy to posh and expensive. Market trends show a reduction in the number of available hotel rooms because developers can use the land more lucratively for office space. Even some Hong Kong landmarks are now in danger. For the traveler, this means higher prices and less availability for any range of accommodation.

For the most part, it's best to plan ahead for budget-minded travelers going to Hong Kong. Hostels and guest houses fill up very quickly, and the time it takes to make a few phone calls will avoid the inconvenience of dragging your luggage around town searching for a place to lay your head.

One contact is the **Hong Kong Youth Hostels Association** (HKYHA, ☎ 788 1638). For HK$60, they will sell IYHF cards and a member's handbook highlighting hostels in Hong Kong. Most hostels cost HK$25 a night and are closed between 10 a.m. and 4 p.m. Many have an 11 p.m. curfew. Advance booking is required at some, but recommended at all locations.

Chungking Mansions
30 Nathan Road
Kowloon, HONG KONG

Seedy and decrepit, Chungking Mansions defies logic in its ability to attract international budget travelers. Yet for years it has been the quintessential meeting place of the backpacker set. Recent reports show an upsurge in crime here, due in large part to illegal immigration from the mainland. Even though every other guidebook recommends Chungking Mansions, we suggest that you attempt to find lodging elsewhere. Nonetheless, a stay in Chungking Mansions puts one right in the heart of Kowloon. Crowds, pollution and shops selling everything under the sun are quite abundant in this area. Prices are rising sharply of late, as the guesthouses struggle to comply with new city codes.

Longtime residents of Hong Kong suggest staying in the upper or lower floors for quick exit to fresh air in case of fire. The following are some recommendations in "A" Block which meet these specifications: **The Traveler's Hostel**, on the 16th Floor was renovated in the early 1990s and has relatively good security. This hostel has been popular for years, and is a good place to network with other travelers. Accommodations run HK$40-130 for dormitories, and double rooms with or without a bathroom. **Sky Guest House** (☎ 368 3767), on the 3rd floor, is one of the cheapest and dirtiest places to stay in Hong Kong. Dormitory beds run about HK$40. The biggest plus, of course, is it's a very short walk up the stairs—and down.

Staying on the Kowloon side and moving up a bit on the price scale, the **Mirador Mansions** at 58 Nathan Road is a cleaner, smaller version of the notorious Chungking Mansions. The **Man Hing Lung Guesthouse**, on the 14th Floor (☎ 722-0678) is very clean and has singles and doubles available for HK$160 per night. Management will match up single travelers, which will reduce the price to HK$80 each. All rooms have a private bath, air conditioning and television.

Hostels, guest houses and dormitories are not restricted to the Kowloon side of the harbor, however. They are plentiful on Hong Kong Island as well. A bit out of the way, but clean and quiet, the **Ma Wui Hall Youth Hostel** (☎ 817 5715) comes highly recommended. With great harbor views from atop Mount Davis near Kennedy Town on the Western part of Hong Kong Island, the HK$25 nightly price tag is a great bargain. Getting there can be a bit rough: From the airport, take the A2 bus to Central, then change to the 5B or 47. From the bus stop, walk back 100 meters and look for the YHA sign and follow the road up the hill. There is a well-marked shortcut. The walk from the bus stop to the hostel takes about 30 minutes, so if you can't climb the hill with your baggage you may need to take a taxi to the top.

In the middle price range, the **Harbor View International House** (1 MacDonnell Road in Central) rents clean, comfortable doubles for HK$480–580, and is in a safe and relatively convenient location. The peak tram station is not far and the Central business district is a short walk down some very steep steps. The 12A bus, an air-conditioned double decker which stops near the hotel, is a quick, easy, and relatively inexpensive (about HK$4) way to get to the heart of Central.

CHEAP EATS

Temple Street Night Market

Hundreds of stalls are set up each night, mostly by vendors of bargain clothes, jewelry, and other factory seconds. These vendors have to eat, so other vendors run food stalls at the north end of the market. Find a stall that looks popular, sit down, and point at whatever looks good. You can't find cheaper food this side of Marrakesh. Indian, Indonesian and Philippine cuisines complement the local Cantonese fare. Open approximately 8pm to 11pm. Recent reports have pickpockets plying their trade here (and in any other crowded place in the world), so be smart. Take the MTR to the Jordan Road Station, and follow the signs for the Temple Street Exit.

City Hall Dim Sum

City Hall Low Block
Edinburgh Place
Central, HONG KONG

Dim Sum (stuffed dumplings, usually fried or steamed) is one of Hong Kong's specialties—and the City Hall is among the locals' favorite places to sample it. It is traditionally served on trolleys. There's not a lot of English spoken here, so you just point at what you want as the trolleys cruise past you. Tables fill up and all the trolleys empty very fast, so it is best to arrive early—in most cases before 11. No reservations, all major credit cards accepted, casual attire. Open 10am to 2pm.

The next two are slightly more upscale options:

The American Restaurant

20 Lockhart Road,
Wanchai, HONG KONG
☎ 527 1000

The American Restaurant (originally named as such to lure American sailors) is something of a Hong Kong tradition. It has been serving top-quality Peking cuisine at bargain-basement prices since just after World War II. Specialties include Peking Duck and Beggars Chicken (both dishes are a bit more expensive but compared to most establishments a great value here). Chili prawns on a sizzling plate are another excellent choice. Fixed-price meals are available at lunch. Reservations recommended, casual attire. Two can eat well here for HK$200. Lunch from 11am, dinner until 11:15pm. No credit cards.

Carrianna

2/F Hilton Tower, 96 Granville Road
Tsimshatsui East, Kowloon, HONG KONG
☎ 724 4828

An excellent value for the local specialty—Chiu Chow cuisine. The high-priced luxury dishes such as Shark's Fin are to be avoided, but try the baby oysters in scrambled eggs. Some excellent dim sum dishes are also available. Casual dress. Lunch from 11:30am to 3pm, dinner from 5pm to 11:30pm. Credit cards accepted, reservations recommended. Set meals available at lunch and dinner. Two people can eat too much for HK$300. There is a second location at 151 Gloucester Road in Wanchai.

TO & FROM THE AIRPORT

The Airbus airport shuttles depart from just outside the arrivals area, running every 15 minutes from 7am to midnight. There are three separate routes: the A1 goes to Tsimshatsui in Kowloon, passing the Chungking Mansions and going out to the Star Ferry. The A2 serves Wanchai, Central, and the Macau Ferry Terminal. The A3 heads out to Causeway Bay. The Airbus stops at major hotels as well as posted bus stops, and costs HK$8-12.

UNIQUELY HONG KONG

The outlying islands present a host of adventures for travelers, and reveal a whole different side of Hong Kong. Most are accessible by ferry in under an hour. Ferry schedules are available at the Star Ferry terminal on both sides of the harbor.

Lantau Island offers several options. From the island's ferry terminal, you can take Bus #2 to the **Po Lin Monastery**, home of a gigantic statue of Buddha and a wonderful hiking path. The bus ride is a white-knuckle affair along narrow, windy roads, but it's worth it. The hiking path—up toward Lantau Peak—is very steep and only recommended for those in excellent health. From the peak, the views of Lantau Harbor and back toward Buddha are certainly worth the climb. Lunch at the monastery is vegetarian style, since no meat is allowed on the grounds. Another option is to take Bus #1 from the Lantau Ferry terminal. This bus goes to the **Tai O** fishing village. Step off the bus, and walk into old Hong Kong, the kind of place most travelers have only seen in black-and-white postcards.

Bridges Worldwide

Room 908, Pacific Trade Center

2 Kaihing Road

Kowloon Bay, HONG KONG

☎ 305 1412, 305 1413

Fax 795 8312

Times to Call: 9:30am to 5:30pm

Type of Provider: Courier company

Areas of Specialty: Worldwide

DESTINATIONS	SAMPLE ROUND TRIP FARE	STANDARD ECONOMY FARE	LENGTH OF STAY
Bangkok	HK$1,000	HK$4,120	up to 21 days
London	HK$5,000	HK$14,670	up to 45 days
Manila	HK$900	HK$2,840	up to 30 days
San Francisco	HK$4,800	HK$13,380	up to one year
Sydney	HK$6,500	HK$13,880	6 to 60 days
Toronto	HK$6,800	HK$18,960	up to 30 days
Vancouver	HK$4,800	HK$15,380	up to 30 days

Payment Methods: Cash, money order, certified check, personal check

Courier Duties on Return Trip: Yes

Minimum Age: 18 years

In Business Since: 1989

Recommended Advance Reservations: 3 months

One-way tickets are available to Bangkok, San Francisco and Sydney. There are two flights per day to Bangkok, which is convenient if you are traveling with a companion. Call to check on last-minute discounts and free flights! This company maintains a cancellation phone list. Flights on Canadian, Gulf Air, Qantas, and Thai Air.

Bangkok, London, Manila, and Sydney flights allow you to bring 20 kilograms of checked luggage. The San Francisco flight allows checked luggage on the return portion of the flight only.

Hong Kong Student Travel

1812 Argyle Centre, Phase 1
688 Nathan Road
Kowloon, HONG KONG
☎ 390 0421, 721 3269
Fax 725 3847

Times to Call: 10am to 7:30pm, 10am to 6:30pm Saturday, 12pm
to 5pm Sunday
Type of Provider: Discount travel agency
Areas of Specialty: Worldwide

DESTINATIONS	SAMPLE ROUND TRIP FARE	STANDARD ECONOMY FARE
Bangkok	HK$1,900	HK$4,120
London	HK$6,150	HK$14,670
Los Angeles	HK$5,500	HK$11,680
New York	HK$7,600	HK$22,960
Sydney	HK$6,300	HK$13,880
Tokyo	HK$4,140	HK$6,420

Payment Methods: Cash, money order, certified check, personal
check, Visa, MasterCard
In Business Since: 1975

HKST has several offices throughout Hong Kong, all of which are
members of the STA Travel Network. STA is the world's largest travel
organization for students and young, independent travelers. They
have 120 locations worldwide. Some of their best fares require student ID, or carry a maximum age.

Their tickets are highly flexible, usually good for one year and requiring no advance purchase. Date changes can be made at any office
worldwide for $25; refunds cost only $50 to $75. Such flexible tick-
ets are a wise choice for travelers going on long trips without fully
concrete itineraries. STA tickets are priced based on one-way travel,
which makes it easy to book open-jaw flights.

Jupiter Air Ltd.

Room 1701, Tower One
China Hong Kong City
33 Canton Road
Kowloon, HONG KONG
☎ 735 1946
Fax 735 0450

Times to Call: 9am to 5:30pm weekdays, 9am to 1pm Saturday
Type of Provider: Courier company
Areas of Specialty: Worldwide

DESTINATIONS	SAMPLE ROUND TRIP FARE	STANDARD ECONOMY FARE	LENGTH OF STAY
Bangkok	HK$800	HK$4,120	up to 14 days
London	HK$5,000	HK$14,670	up to 30 days
Los Angeles	HK$3,800	HK$11,680	up to 30 days
New York	HK$5,000	HK$22,960	up to 30 days
Sydney	HK$6,500	HK$13,880	up to 30 days
Tokyo	HK$1,800	HK$6,420	up to 30 days
Vancouver	HK$5,000	HK$15,380	up to 30 days

Payment Methods: Cash, money order, certified check, personal check
Deposit: Normally HK$1,000. No deposit for Sydney; HK$2,000 for Bangkok
Courier Duties on Return Trip: Yes
Minimum Age: 18 years
In Business Since: 1988

Call on the first day of the month, two months ahead of time, in order to reserve a flight. For example, for October flights you must call on August 1st. On August 2, there will be very few of these great deals left. At press time, there were two flights per day to New York. One-way tickets are available to Sydney for HK$3,800 and to Tokyo for HK$1,000. This company maintains a cancellation phone list.

Flights to London and Sydney are on Qantas; to North America and Japan on Japan Airlines and United Airlines; to Bangkok on Thai Airways.

The prices listed apply to the months of February, July, August and September. The rest of the year, tickets are about HK$500 cheaper.

Current prices appear in ads in the *South China Morning Post.*

Linehaul Express / Sophia Lai

Room 2209-B Tower One
33 Canton Road
Kowloon, HONG KONG
☎ 735 2163, 735 2167, 736 2769
Fax 735 1372
Contact: Matthew Chan

Times to Call: 9:30am to 5:30pm
Type of Provider: Courier company
Areas of Specialty: Worldwide

DESTINATIONS	SAMPLE ROUND TRIP FARE	STANDARD ECONOMY FARE	LENGTH OF STAY
Bangkok	HK$1,500	HK$4,120	3 to 14 days
Frankfurt	HK$7,800	HK$21,500	10 to 30 days
London	HK$6,800	HK$14,670	7 to 30 days
Manchester	HK$7,200	HK$16,470	7 to 30 days
Manila	HK$800	HK$2,840	3 to 10 days
Singapore	HK$2,100	HK$6,660	4 to 30 days
Sydney	HK$6,200	HK$13,880	7 to 30 days
Taipei	HK$900	HK$3,000	4 to 30 days
Tokyo	HK$2,000	HK$6,420	5 to 14 days

Payment Methods: Cash, check, Visa
Deposit: HK$2,000
Courier Duties on Return Trip: Yes
Minimum Age: 18 years
In Business Since: 1989
Recommended Advance Reservations: 2 to 3 months

Because Linehaul Express is the general sales agent for Cathay Pacific Wholesale Courier, all flights are on Cathay Pacific Airlines. Additional offices are located in Frankfurt and London.

One-way tickets are available. Call to check on last-minute discounts. This company maintains a cancellation phone list.

Major Travel (Hong Kong) Co.

Room 301, Lap Fai Building
6-8 Pottinger Street
Central, HONG KONG
☎ 526 9226
Fax 521 6797

Times to Call: 9am to 5pm
Type of Provider: Consolidator
Areas of Specialty: Worldwide

DESTINATIONS	SAMPLE ROUND TRIP FARE	STANDARD ECONOMY FARE
Bangkok	HK$2,200	HK$4,120
London	HK$6,950	HK$14,670
Los Angeles	HK$6,100	HK$11,680
New York	HK$7,600	HK$22,960
Sydney	HK$6,900	HK$13,880

Payment Methods: Cash, money order, certified check, personal
check, Visa, MasterCard, American Express
In Business Since: 1982

Prestige Travel

8th Floor, Jubilee Commercial Building
42-46 Gloucester Road
Wan Chai, HONG KONG
☎ 528 6006
Fax 861 2150

Times to Call: 9am to 6pm
Type of Provider: Consolidator
Areas of Specialty: Europe and Asia

DESTINATIONS	SAMPLE ROUND TRIP FARE	STANDARD ECONOMY FARE
Bangkok	HK$1,900	HK$4,120
London	HK$7,020	HK$14,670
Los Angeles	HK$6,800	HK$11,680
Paris	HK$7,600	HK$21,500
Sydney	HK$7,200	HK$13,880
Tokyo	HK$8,700	HK$6,420

Payment Methods: Cash, check, Visa, MasterCard

In Business Since: 1984

Prestige works with both business and student travelers. They have chosen to remain small in order to offer better service and lower prices.

Travelers Hostel Travel Agency

16th Floor, A Block, Chungking Mansions
Kowloon, HONG KONG
☎ 368 7710

Times to Call: 9am to 5pm
Type of Provider: Consolidator
Areas of Specialty: Worldwide

DESTINATIONS	SAMPLE ROUND TRIP FARE	STANDARD ECONOMY FARE
Bangkok	HK$1,780	HK$4,120
London	HK$6,800	HK$14,670
Los Angeles	HK$6,150	HK$11,680
New York	HK$7,250	HK$22,960
Sydney	HK$6,750	HK$13,880
Tokyo	HK$5,800	HK$6,420

Payment Methods: Cash, check, Visa
In Business Since: 1979

This agency is part of the Traveler's Hostel in the Chungking Mansions, and comes highly recommended.

SINGAPORE

MARKET TRENDS

Singapore used to be a major center of ticket exporting; now, Singapore agencies import tickets issued elsewhere. Times really have changed. It is important to note that the price for tickets in Singapore and Malaysia is often the same dollar amount; depending on the value of each currency, you may get a much better deal by buying in Malaysia. Garuda Indonesia airlines reliably offers some of the best deals out of Singapore.

But your best bet out of Singapore is catching a courier flight, usually to other Asian destinations, but sometimes to London. Pick up a copy of the *Straits Times* to get a feel for the latest airfare prices. Beware of the exit airport tax, for which you must reserve S$12 cash to pay at the airport on your way home. Customs officials will accept "sufficient funds" in lieu of the onward tickets normally required to enter the country.

STOPPING OVER IN SINGAPORE

Singapore is a well-functioning, thriving metropolis. One visitor refers to it as "Chicago on an island." Most activities for the visitor involve shopping or eating. Beaches and similar areas of natural beauty are harder to find.

Singapore is stiflingly clean, approaching dull, some would say. But beyond the tourist-ridden plazas of Orchard Road, those who stop to look will find a hidden charm which makes a visit worthwhile. Behind the skyscraper-laden Western facade of the commercial sector lies a strong Asian culture rooted in Confucian traditions. Venture into Chinatown or Little India to catch a glimpse of Singapore with its guard down.

The climate is consistently hot and sticky, year around. During the November–January monsoon season, Singapore is slightly cooler, albeit much wetter. The heat does not seem unbearable amidst the air-conditioned buildings, taxis, stores, buses and MRTs (Mass Rapid Transit subways). Like everything else in Singapore, public transit is clean and efficient.

TELEPHONE COUNTRY CODE:

(65)

CURRENCY:
Singaporean Dollar
US$1.00 = S$1.33

Singapore is a prime example of redevelopment gone out of control. Even the infamous Raffles Hotel was nearly demolished to make way for more office towers. Finding the need to modernize irresistible, developers decided to transform the rescued Raffles from an unpretentious colonial hotel into an opulent, super-luxury operation. Drop in to try a Singapore Sling (which was first concocted here), but stay somewhere else unless you have a large inheritance to burn.

A note on bargaining: if a vendor asks, tell him you are staying at the youth hostel. Vendors are not asking out of friendly curiosity; they simply need to know how much money you have. They will quote much higher prices for shoppers saying at the Raffles than those staying at hostels. Bargaining is expected everywhere except in department stores. Tipping is not expected.

Oh, yeah. Obey the law in Singapore. Don't spit, don't litter, don't chew gum. Do use crosswalks, flush, and smile at the ubiquitous police. By meticulously conforming, you will prevent your trip from coming to, er, a painful end. . . .

CHEAP SLEEPS

Bencoolen Street is home to many of Singapore's best budget lodging opportunities. Conveniently located near the Queen Street Terminal, this neighborhood is also pleasantly far from the Orchard Road tourist traps.

Goh's Homestay
169 D Bencoolen Street, 6th Floor
Singapore
☎ 339 6561
Fax 339 8606

Basic, air-conditioned rooms. In the same building are the Hawaii Guesthouse on the 2nd Floor, and Philip Choo's on the 3rd Floor. Dorm rooms S$12, singles S$36, doubles S$46.

Hotel Bencoolen
47 Bencoolen Street
Singapore
☎ 336 0822

In the moderate price category, this is a pleasant, small hotel. All rooms have A/C and private bath. Center rooms, either singles or doubles, cost S$94. Deluxe rooms are about S$10 more. Complimentary breakfast.

YMCA International House
1 Orchard Road
Singapore
☎ 337 3444
Fax 337 3140

If you must be in the middle of the Orchard Road madness, this is the cheap place to stay. The Y is a functional, practical, hotel-like place, with a rooftop swimming pool, billiards room and health club. All rooms have A/C and private baths. Dorm beds are S$23, singles are S$75, and doubles are S$85.

CHEAP EATS

Hawker centers are clearly a best buy. Working-class folks stop in for delicious, authentic fare in a food-stall atmosphere. Tourists do not frequent such establishments, but true travelers relish the opportunity to share a table with the locals. Order dishes from multiple, ethnically diverse stalls, depending on what looks good. Well-known hawker centers can be found at **The Satay Club** (on Queen Elizabeth Walk, a few blocks towards the waterfront from Raffles), **Paradiz Centre** (Selegie Road near Bencoolen), and **Newton Circus** (the trendy crowd congregates here at night, near Newton MTR stop).

Fatty's, on Albert Street near Bencoolen, serves up cheap but high-quality Cantonese fare. The jolly chef Fatty opened this place when the government decided that food stalls (including Fatty's) no longer fit the Official Plan for Albert Street. The change in locale has done nothing but improve his popularity.

TO & FROM THE AIRPORT

Catch bus #390 from Basement 2. Fare is S$1.30; exact change required. The ride to the city center takes about 45 minutes. Buses run every 15 minutes, from 6am to 11:45pm. The bus will drop you off at the Queen Street Terminal on Rochor Road, which is a good area for budget lodgings. Bus No. 16 or 16/Express is another option, running from the airport to the corner of Bras Basah and Bencoolen Streets.

UNIQUELY SINGAPORE

Hidden Singapore is very well hidden; ask locals who look like they might know for the latest word-of-mouth tips. One place to get away from the air-conditioning (so as to regain an appreciation for it, of course) is the **Bukit Timah Nature Reserve**, on Upper Bukit Timah Road. This sprawling expanse of primary jungle has predictably well-kept trails.

Air United

5002 Beach Road, No. 03-64E
Golden Mile Complex
Singapore 0719
☎ 294 5954
Fax 294 6094
Contact: Karen Ho

Times to Call: 9am to 5pm
Type of Provider: Courier company
Areas of Specialty: Worldwide

DESTINATIONS	SAMPLE ROUND TRIP FARE	STANDARD ECONOMY FARE	LENGTH OF STAY
Bangkok	S$220	S$1,112	up to 14 days
London	S$1,300	S$3,648	up to 3 mos.
Los Angeles	S$900	S$5,272	up to 30 days
San Francisco	S$900	S$5,272	up to 30 days
Taipei	S$500	S$2,454	up to 30 days
Tokyo	tba	S$3,140	up to 30 days

Payment Methods: Cash, check
Deposit: S$200
Courier Duties on Return Trip: Yes
Minimum Age: 18 years
In Business Since: 1989
Recommended Advance Reservations: 1 month

Call to check on last-minute discounts. All destinations except Taipei
allow 20 kilograms of checked luggage.

Airtropolis Express

Fook Hai Building, Basement 1, B1-09
Singapore 0104
☎ 543 1934
Fax 545 2055
Contact: S. K.

Times to Call: 9am to 6pm
Type of Provider: Courier company
Areas of Specialty: Asia

DESTINATIONS	SAMPLE ROUND TRIP FARE	STANDARD ECONOMY FARE	LENGTH OF STAY
Bangkok	S$200	S$1,112	4 to 5 days
Bangkok	S$290	S$1,112	up to 14 days
Hong Kong	S$450	1,892	7 days

Payment Methods: Cash only
Courier Duties on Return Trip: Yes
Minimum Age: 18 years
In Business Since: 1989
Recommended Advance Reservations: 2 weeks

Call to check on last-minute discounts.

Bridges Worldwide

SATS Air Freight Terminal, Module 1A
Second Floor, Room 203
Changi Airport, Singapore 1781
☎ 545 4327
Fax 543 0258

Times to Call: 9:30am to 5:30pm
Type of Provider: Courier company
Areas of Specialty: Worldwide

DESTINATIONS	SAMPLE ROUND TRIP FARE	STANDARD ECONOMY FARE	LENGTH OF STAY
Bangkok	S$200	S$1,112	up to 14 days

Payment Methods: Cash only
Courier Duties on Return Trip: Yes
Minimum Age: 18 years
In Business Since: 1989
Recommended Advance Reservations: 2 weeks

Call to check on last-minute discounts and free flights! This company maintains a cancellation phone list.

Many flights allow you to bring 20 kilograms of checked luggage. Hong Kong, London, Manila, San Francisco, Sydney, have been offered as courier destinations from Singapore in the past, and may be available again in 1995.

CIEE Travel

110D Killiney Road

Tai Wah Building

Singapore 0923

☎ 738 7066

Fax 733 7421

Times to Call: 9am to 5:30pm weekdays, 8:30am to 1pm Saturday

Type of Provider: Discount travel agent

Areas of Specialty: Worldwide

DESTINATIONS	SAMPLE ROUND TRIP FARE	STANDARD ECONOMY FARE
Bangkok	$S305	S$1,112
London	$S1,550	S$3,648
New York	$S2,100	S$6,360
Sydney	$S700	S$2,792

In Business Since: 1947

Payment Methods: Cash, money order, personal check, Visa, MasterCard, American Express

Open from 10am to 2pm Saturdays, for walk-in clients only.

(See the Council Travel listing in the Chicago chapter for company background.)

Gasi Travel

12 Devonshire Road

Singapore 0923

☎ 235 9900

Fax 738 3767

Times to Call: 9am to 5:30pm

Type of Provider: Consolidator

Areas of Specialty: Worldwide, including around-the-world

DESTINATIONS	SAMPLE ROUND TRIP FARE	STANDARD ECONOMY FARE
London	S$1,923	S$3,648
Los Angeles	S$1,700	S$5,272
New York	S$2,250	S$6,360
Paris	S$2,033	S$3,458

| Singapore | Sydney | S$1,288 | S$2,792 |
| | Tokyo | S$1,571 | S$3,140 |

Payment Methods: Cash, check, Visa
In Business Since: 1972

Gasi imports tickets from all over the world, and can get you some of the cheapest flights out of Singapore.

STA Travel

2-17 Orchard Parade Hotel
1 Tanglin Road
Singapore 1024
☎ 734 5681
Fax 737 2591

Times to Call: 9am to 5pm weekdays, 9am to 12pm Saturday
Type of Provider: Discount travel agency
Areas of Specialty: Worldwide

DESTINATIONS	SAMPLE ROUND TRIP FARE	STANDARD ECONOMY FARE
Bangkok	S$300	S$1,112
London	S$1,070	S$3,648
Los Angeles	S$1,320	S$5,272
New York	S$1,420	S$6,360
Paris	S$1,480	S$3,458
Tokyo	S$1,018	S$3,140

Payment Methods: Cash, money order, certified check, personal check, Visa, MasterCard, American Express
In Business Since: 1975

There is a small surcharge for credit card transactions.

STA is the world's largest travel organization for students and young, independent travelers. They have 120 locations worldwide. Some of their best fares require student ID, or carry a maximum age.

Their tickets are highly flexible, usually good for one year and requiring no advance purchase. Date changes can be made at any office worldwide for $25; refunds cost only $50 to $75. Such flexible tickets are a wise choice for travelers going on long trips without fully concrete itineraries. STA tickets are priced based on one-way tickets, which makes it easy to book open-jaw flights.

TNT Skypak

1 Shenton Way
Robina House, 18th Floor
Singapore 1806
☎ 222 7255
Fax 225 1654
Contact: Vicki or Eileen

Times to Call: 8:30am to 5:30pm
Type of Provider: Courier company
Areas of Specialty: Worldwide

DESTINATIONS	SAMPLE ROUND TRIP FARE	STANDARD ECONOMY FARE	LENGTH OF STAY
Los Angeles	S$1,050	S$5,272	up to 3 weeks

Payment Methods: Cash, certified check, personal check, Visa, MasterCard, American Express
Courier Duties on Return Trip: Yes
Minimum Age: 18 years
In Business Since: 1991
Recommended Advance Reservations: 1 to 2 months

Call to check on last-minute discounts. This company also maintains a standby phone list. First-time TNT couriers are sometimes allowed to be on the standby list, "if they are very sincere." All flights are on Northwest Airlines.

SYDNEY, AUSTRALIA

MARKET TRENDS

CHAPTER 15

For Those Headed Out of Australia

Standard airfares are painfully expensive in Australia. Even after deregulation, government capacity controls and pricy bilateral agreements set international fares so high, Aussies must often travel for a year or two at a time in order to justify the expense of airfare. Long distances within Australia combined with the small population make it difficult for new airlines to survive, let alone challenge the established airlines.

Fortunately, there are plenty of courier flights out of Australia, and they are very poorly publicized. It shouldn't be difficult to book a courier flight for the dates you want at a price you won't believe.

If you are unable to find a courier flight that suits your needs, your best bet is to shop around Sydney's consolidators. In addition to the listings in this chapter, cheap flights are always advertised in the weekend papers. Check out Saturday's *Melbourne Age* or the Sydney *Morning Herald*.

For Those Headed to Australia

You're best off purchasing internal airfares for Australia before you arrive. Your international round trip ticket qualifies you for the air pass programs of both Ansett and Qantas, which offer domestic flights at fares dramatically cheaper than those otherwise available. But once you've arrived in the country/continent, it is too late to buy an air pass (for details, see Appendix A: Air Pass Programs). Note that everyone except citizens of Australia and New Zealand needs a visa and an onward ticket to get into Australia.

For bed and breakfasts, cruises, and tours, take advantage of standby rates. By waiting until the last-minute, you can often get great deals if there is space available. Check the bulletin boards at each city's tourist office, or use the telephone book and call around. Savings of 50 percent or more are common.

STOPPING OVER IN SYDNEY

Situated around three spectacular harbors, Sydney was an obvious

TELEPHONE COUNTRY CODE:
(61)

CURRENCY:
Australian Dollar
US$1.00 = AU$1.23

choice for one of Australia's first settlements. From humble beginnings as a convict colony to host city of the 2000 Olympic Games, Sydney has claimed an international reputation as one of the world's most beautiful cities.

If your mental image of Australia is of Ayers Rock and the Outback, Sydney will astonish you. It's a fast-paced, sophisticated and multicultural city. Sydney's own blend of natural beauty and outstanding architecture characterizes a city which has something for everyone.

Sydney Harbor sparkles. A blue sky creates an immaculate back drop for viewing the city's unique skyline and world-famous harbor. The **Opera House** and bridge are best viewed from the water. Take the Manly Ferry from Circular Quay for AU$3.40. Enjoy the 30-minute ride, after which you will find yourself at one of Sydney's most famous beaches.

On the South Side, **Bondi Beach** is worth a visit for its fantastic selection of restaurants, cafés, and cosmopolitan beach life, especially on weekends.

The area between Circular Quay and the Harbor Bridge is known as **The Rocks**, and no tour of Sydney is complete without a walk around these historic streets. This is the site where the First Fleet chose to land and establish Britain's first outpost in Australia. Pick up a tour map from the **Rocks Visitors Centre** (104 George Street) and you can explore on foot.

CHEAP SLEEPS

The main concentration of hostels is in and around **Kings Cross**. Apart from being a lively red light district, Kings Cross is a melting pot of back packers, 24-hour bars, and unusual characters.

The Traveler's Rest
156 Victoria Street
Sydney, NSW 2011 AUSTRALIA
☎ (02) 358 4606

Dorm beds with cooking facilities for AU$14. There are televisions in every room. Run by a family who lives on the premises. They pride themselves on being the cleanest hostel in Kings Cross. They are very helpful, and can even assist travelers who want to find work.

The Down Under Hostel
25 Hughes Street
Potts Point, Sydney, NSW 2011 AUSTRALIA
☎ (02) 358 1143
Fax 02/ 357 4675

The Down Under was the first hostel opened in Sydney, and remains one of the biggest. It is a good place for meeting people. Dorm beds go for AU$14; weekly rates and twin rooms are available.

For a more relaxed stay, close to the beach, try:

Coogee Beach Backpackers
94 Beach Street
Coogee, NSW 2034 AUSTRALIA
☎ (02) 665 7735
Fax 02/ 664 1258

Dorm beds for AU$12. The staff is quite friendly. They organize a barbecue and volleyball game on the beach every Sunday.

CHEAP EATS

If you have the time to sample a few cafés and restaurants, invest in the thorough **Cheap Eats Guide** for AU$8, available from most news agencies.

Budget travelers will have little trouble finding cheap meals in the Kings Cross area. Many restaurants are geared towards them. For instance, try **Kellets Restaurant** at 13 Kellet Way, where you'll find pasta for AU$3.50 a plate.

For cheap Italian food, bustling breakfasts, and a lively street scene, head to **Stanley Street**, East Sydney. One of the best restaurants is **Bill and Toni's** (74 King Street), where huge servings are the rule. Newtown has Sydney's best selection of inexpensive cafés and restaurants aimed at a student budget. **El Bamsa** at 233 King has the best coffee. **Café Stromboli**'s glass-roofed courtyard is an oasis of serenity at 134 King.

TO & FROM THE AIRPORT

All of the hostels listed above have an airport pickup service. Check the board and use the free telephone at the airport. Also, an airport express bus operates from Circular Quay every 20 minutes for AU$5, or AU$8 roundtrip if you plan ahead.

UNIQUELY SYDNEY

Art fans will fall in love with **Paddington**, a hip, inner-city suburb where most of Sydney's galleries thrive in the midst of newly renovated terraces and classy pubs. Check out the art-and-craft market held every Saturday at the corner of Newcombe and Oxford Streets.

Stretching from Paddington back towards the city is **Oxford Street**. In late February, Oxford Street explodes into action with Sydney's gay and lesbian Mardi Gras. The rest of the year, this area offers a vast array of pubs and clubs which draws a hip, mixed crowd. **The Freezer** at 11 Oxford Street has the latest dance mixes and draws a younger clientele.

To escape the inner city, the closest beach is in **Bondi**. Take buses No. 380 or 382 from Circular Quay. Sunday is the best day to visit if you enjoy promenading along waterfronts, dodging roller bladers, and listening to South American drummers and other buskers. Reggae bands play at the **Surf Pavilion** in the afternoons, further contributing to the cosmopolitan mayhem of Bondi Beach. For better surfing and more secluded beaches, take the bus from Manly Wharf towards Palm Beach (along the Northern Peninsula), stopping at Whale or Bungan beaches.

Jupiter Air

10 Spring Street
PO Box 1219
Bondi Junction, NSW 2022 AUSTRALIA
☎ (02) 369 2704
Fax 02/ 369 3682

Times to Call: 9am to 4pm, Monday through Thursday
Type of Provider: Courier company
Areas of Specialty: Worldwide

DESTINATIONS	SAMPLE ROUND TRIP FARE	STANDARD ECONOMY FARE	LENGTH OF STAY
Auckland	AU$285	AU$1,042	7 to 10 days
London	AU$1,600	AU$2,449	up to 3 mos.
Los Angeles	AU$850	AU$2,820	up to 30 days

Payment Methods: Cash, bank check, personal check
Luggage: One checked bag plus carry-ons
Courier duties: Both to and from destination
In Business Since: 1988
Recommended Advance Reservations: 1 to 3 months

London flights can be booked from either Melbourne or Sydney. One-way tickets are sometimes available. Flights are substantially pricier in high season, rising to about AU$1,800 return for London. The company stresses that the fares quoted above are only samples, and that prices are always changing. Jupiter Air is now the biggest courier company operating out of Australia.

Phil Travel

6th Floor
105 Pitt Street
Sydney, 2000 AUSTRALIA
☎ (02) 232 5677
Fax 02/ 235 3142

Times to Call: 9am to 5pm
Type of Provider: Discount travel agency
Areas of Specialty: Worldwide

DESTINATIONS	SAMPLE ROUND TRIP FARE	STANDARD ECONOMY FARE
Bangkok	AU$735	AU$1,772
London	AU$1,530	AU$2,449
Los Angeles	AU$1,220	AU$2,820
New York	AU$1,630	AU$6,566
Paris	AU$1,530	AU$2,640
Tokyo	AU$1,100	AU$3,902

Payment Methods: Cash, Visa, MasterCard, American Express
In Business Since: 1984

Clients who are serious about getting the cheapest available air tickets are supplied with a market research form. Phil Travel is so confident that they can get you the cheapest fare, they encourage you to fill out the form and use it to shop around at other agencies. If you find a quote that they cannot match or better, they will give you AU$50 upon proof of purchase.

Polo Express

PO Box 457
Mascot, NSW 2020 AUSTRALIA
☎ (02) 666 4655
Fax 02/ 666 3387

Times to Call: 9:30am to 4pm
Type of Provider: Courier company
Areas of Specialty: Worldwide

DESTINATIONS	SAMPLE ROUND TRIP FARE	STANDARD ECONOMY FARE	LENGTH OF STAY
Auckland	AU$350	AU$1,042	varies
London	tba	AU$2,449	varies

Payment Methods: Cash, money order, certified check
Courier Duties on Return Trip: No
In Business Since: 1990
Recommended Advance Reservations: 3 to 4 months
Luggage: One checked bag (max. 44 lbs / 20 kgs) and one carry-on

Call for last-minute discounts. Polo keeps a cancellation phone list. Couriers on the Auckland flight can return any time from Christchurch, Wellington, or Auckland. Flights run five times per week.

Student Travel Australia (STA)

732 Harris Street, First Floor

Ultimo, NSW 2007 AUSTRALIA

☎ (02) 281 9866

Fax 02/ 281 4183

Times to Call: 9am to 5pm

Type of Provider: Discount travel agency

Areas of Specialty: Worldwide

DESTINATIONS	SAMPLE ROUND TRIP FARE	STANDARD ECONOMY FARE
Bangkok	AU$750	AU$1,772
London	AU$1,630	AU$2,449
Los Angeles	AU$1,495	AU$2,820
New York	AU$2,135	AU$6,566
Paris	AU$1,630	AU$2,640
Tel Aviv	AU$1,780	n/a
Tokyo	AU$1,220	AU$3,902

Payment Methods: Cash, Visa, MasterCard, American Express

In Business Since: 1975

STA is the world's largest travel organization for students and young, independent travelers. They have 120 locations worldwide, including several in Sydney and Melbourne. Some of their best fares require student ID, or carry a maximum age. If you need a student or youth card, they can issue one for you. We used the student card to get into the Acropolis for free, saving AU$12 each.

Their tickets are highly flexible, usually good for one year and requiring no advance purchase. Date changes can be made at any office worldwide for $25; refunds cost only $50 to $75. Such flexible tickets are a wise choice for travelers going on long trips without fully concrete itineraries. STA tickets are priced based on one-way tickets, which makes it easy to book open-jaw flights.

Sydney Flight Centre

Shop 524
Gateway Quay Side
1 MacQuarie Street
Sydney 2000 AUSTRALIA
☎ (02) 241 2422
Fax 02/ 241 4113

Times to Call: 9am to 5pm
Type of Provider: Consolidator
Areas of Specialty: Worldwide

DESTINATIONS	SAMPLE ROUND TRIP FARE	STANDARD ECONOMY FARE
Bangkok	AU$760	AU$1,772
London	AU$1,540	AU$2,449
Los Angeles	AU$1,380	AU$2,820
New York	AU$1,670	AU$6,566
Paris	AU$1,540	AU$2,640
Tel Aviv	AU$1,670	n/a
Tokyo	AU$1,120	AU$3,902

Payment Methods: Cash, money order, certified check, personal check
In Business Since: 1980

Consistently one of the cheapest travel agencies in Sydney, with offices all over Australia. Call ☎ (02) 131 600 to speak to the office nearest you.

The company motto is, "we guarantee to beat any genuine quoted price."

The Flight Centre operates many smaller offices, which gives them good buying power while still allowing for very personal service.

TNT Express Worldwide

280 Coward Street
PO Box 351
Mascot, NSW 2020 AUSTRALIA
☎ (02) 317 7717
Fax 02/ 669 3152

Times to Call: 9am to 5:30pm
Type of Provider: Courier company
Areas of Specialty: New Zealand

DESTINATIONS	SAMPLE ROUND TRIP FARE	STANDARD ECONOMY FARE	LENGTH OF STAY
Auckland	AU$350	AU$1,042	Up to 6 mos.

Payment Methods: Cash, bank check, personal check
In Business Since: 1989
Luggage: Varies
Courier Duties on Return Trip: No
One-Way Tickets Available: Yes
Recommended Advance Reservations: 6 to 8 weeks for confirmed seat

Call, listen to the recording, and leave your name and address. An application form with thorough details will be sent to you. You must complete the application before you can book. Send for an application 2 to 3 months before you plan to travel. Return flight can be from Auckland, Christchurch, or Wellington. One-way flights available for AU$200.

Universal Air Couriers

Unit 1, 247 King Street
PO Box 574
Mascot, NSW 2020 AUSTRALIA
☎ (02) 317 5333, 02/ 317 5383
Fax 02/ 317 3061

Times to Call: 9am to 11am
Type of Provider: Courier company
Areas of Specialty: Europe

Sydney

DESTINATIONS	SAMPLE ROUND TRIP FARE	STANDARD ECONOMY FARE	LENGTH OF STAY
London	AU$1,600	AU$2,449	Up to 6 weeks

Payment Methods: Cash, bank check, personal check
Luggage: Two checked bags plus carry-ons
Courier Duties on Return Trip: Yes
In Business Since: 1980
Recommended Advance Reservations: 3 months

One-way tickets are available for AU$1200. Universal demands that its couriers have "no criminal record." All flights are on 100 percent non-smoking Singapore Airlines (don't test them....) Often the courier has nothing to carry, as this seat must be filled every day regardless of shipping needs. The return flight can be via Frankfurt or Amsterdam, and a stopover is permitted. Three flights per week, on Monday, Thursday, and Friday.

TOKYO, JAPAN

CHAPTER 16

MARKET TRENDS

Tokyo is one of the worst places in the world to buy air travel (second only to Saudi Arabia). The combination of high incomes, expense accounts, and government enforcement of IATA fares makes air travel pricy. So why do we even list Tokyo in a book on budget airfares? Because if you lack insider knowledge in this market, you are doomed to pay through the nose for air travel.

Try to have an onward ticket before you arrive in Japan, or buy your ticket abroad, from a San Francisco or London consolidator, and have it mailed to you. (Most foreign tourists need a confirmed onward ticket to get into Japan in the first place.) Courier flights offer genuinely good deals, but you do have to plan ahead. Other than joining the U.S. military, courier flights are the only way to fly cheaply out of Japan. If you can't fly courier, the consolidators listed for Tokyo will give you the best prices available, but that is not saying much. You may also find some ads for discounted tickets in the *Tokyo Journal*.

STOPPING OVER IN TOKYO

Tokyo is a lively if overpopulated city that sprawls like Los Angeles. Unlike Los Angeles, however, most places of interest to travelers can be found inside the ring of the Japan Railways Yamanote line, which circles central Tokyo. Shopping and nightlife are easy to find. Surprisingly, you can also find several historic sites nestled within the starkly modern terrain. Check out the **Senso-ji Temple** in Asakusa, the **Meiji Shrine** across from Harajuku, and the **Imperial Palace**, at the green line's Nijubashimae Station.

To find out what's going on in town, pick up a copy of the English language weeklies *Tokyo Journal* or *Tokyo Time Out*. Orientation in the city is easy. All you need is a subway map, since the entire city is organized around its subway stations. A full street map of the city would be overwhelming. Average subway trips cost ¥120 to ¥200; you pay at the turnstiles. Whenever you get lost (and you will get lost), stop and ask for directions from one of the street-corner police

TELEPHONE COUNTRY CODE:
(81)
CURRENCY:
Dollar
US$1.00 = ¥96

kiosks, known as kobans. Or inquire at Tokyo's **Tourist Information Center,** near Yurakucho Station in Hibiya [☎ (03) 3502 1461].

Ginza is the upscale shopping district; technophiles will love Sony headquarters, where they can browse through several floors of the latest gadgetry. When hunger strikes, pop down into the Ginza train station, where a bowl of curry-rice with egg on top will set you back a mere ¥280.

Young travelers may find **Shinjuku**'s maze of dazzling neon more interesting. In addition to Tokyo's red light and gay districts, Shinjuku boasts some of the trendiest nightclubs, clothing stores, and a collection of electronics bazaars. If you can hear them over the racket of the pachinko parlors, the live bands that perform in the park at the station play everything from jazz to rap. Also near Shinjuku Station is the **Sumitomo Building**, which you can scale for a great view of the city.

In terms of nightlife, **Roppongi** is home to the outrageously expensive international disco and yuppie scene, on the Hibiya line. Look for the famous two-story high King Kong hanging off the side of the Hard Rock Cafe. The only free club in the area is nearby **Gas Panic**, hidden behind a red steel door (it is just past the Mr. Donuts—ask for directions, this place is well known). In the same area, **Club Buzz** is a popular techno dance place. Clubs generally charge a cover of ¥4,000 to ¥8,000, although women sometimes get in for half price. The pink **Almond Restaurant** marks the train station, and is a favorite meeting place for those bound for the Roppongi scene.

The more moderate **Shibuya** digs will still set back your pocketbook a bit, but the area is lively and worth the splurge. There certainly are sleazy clubs looking to fleece tourists in this neighborhood, so avoid the places that try to pull you in, and ask about covers and minimums. In general, Shibuya (Yamanote line) is the young alternative to the red lights and serious, traditional bars of Ginza and Shinjuku. The area is literally overflowing with youth and gaijin (foreigners).

Next to Shibuya, **Harajuku** can best be described as "teeny-bopper land." Come see all the latest adolescent fashions; bell bottoms are hot as of this writing. On Sundays, countless amateur musicians set up shop on the sidewalks.

Few things are cheap in Japan. Accommodations are no exception. Even the YMCA is expensive! Your best budget option is the **Tokyo International Youth Hostel** [18-F Central Plaza Building, 1-1 Kagura-kashi, Shinjuku, Tokyo, JAPAN; ☎ (03) 3235 1107], in the tall glass building outside Iidabashi Station. Dorm beds run about ¥2500 a night.

Ryokan are small, traditional Japanese hotels, complete with tatami mats and futons. The **Kimi Ryokan** [☎ (03) 3971 3766] has gained quite a following among travelers, though it can be a bit tricky to find. Go left at the eastern exit of Ikebukuro Station. Stop at the police koban on the corner, and ask the officer on duty for directions. Singles run ¥3,000 and up; doubles start at ¥5,000. Remember to swap your shoes for the provided slippers upon entering the ryokan, and to remove even the slippers before stepping on the tatami in your room. Some ryokans do not accept foreign guests because foreigners often do not understand the customs. If meals are served, expect the schedule to be rather firm.

You may want to stay in a minshuku, a small, family run inn which can be cheaper than a ryokan, and is the Japanese equivalent of a bed and breakfast. For a list of Japanese lodgings including minshuku, contact the **Welcome Inn Reservation Center** in Tokyo at (03) 3211 4201, or fax them at (03) 3211 9009. Two meals are usually included, and prices run about ¥4,000 a person. You make your own bed, and bring your own towel.

Other budget options include the uniquely Japanese "capsule hotels." These male-only cubicles can be found at train stations and airports. For ¥4,000, you get a locker-like (or coffin-like, depending upon your perspective) space, about one meter high and two meters long, with a bed and a television. Crawl in and get comfortable! One example is the **Ikebukuro Puraza** [☎ (03) 3590 7770], just outside Ikebukuro Station.

If you plan to stay for more than a few days, a gaijin house is the cheapest way to go. Prices start around ¥1500 a night. Both the Tourist Information Center and the weekly magazines have contact information.

CHEAP EATS

Inexpensive restaurants can be found in the basements of most Japanese department stores. Try the one in **Takashimaya**, a large department store near the main shopping district of Ginza, for a basic lunch for about ¥600. This is the kind of place where the Japanese office workers eat, and that's always a good sign for budget travelers. The top three stories of the **Sumitomo Building** (see above) also house working-class restaurants.

A cheap and filling way to eat lunch or dinner on the run is to buy a "bento" (meal in a box) in supermarkets and convenience stores. You can find bentos for about ¥500.

Near the Meguro JR station, **Tonki** [1-1-2 Shimo-Meguro, ☎ (03) 3491 9928] draws a huge local following. The people in line are waiting for tonkatsu, the deep-fried pork cutlet and fixings that this place is famous for. Expect a 15-minute wait to get a table in this frill-free, family run treasure. No reservations, credit cards accepted, meals from ¥1,500.

In the same neighborhood, **Mekong** [Koyo Building 2-F, 2-16-4 Kamiosaki, Shinagawa-ku, ☎ (03) 3442 6664] is a good Southeast Asian restaurant. Spicy Cambodian, Thai, and Vietnamese dishes trail steam all the way from the kitchen to your vinyl-covered table. English menus, reservations accepted.

Noodle bars, yakitori shops, and curry-rice stalls are also good bets for budget eats. Look in the corridors of all major train stations. For example, below the train tracks between Yurakucho Station and Shimbashi is a collection of at least 50 such stalls. At ¥700 yen, ramen can be much more filling than other sometimes dainty Japanese meals.

Shakey's Pizza won't help you assimilate, but you can gorge yourself on their all-you-can-eat lunch specials from 11am to 2pm.

TO & FROM THE AIRPORT

Many trains announce the stops in both English and Japanese, or post signs in both languages inside each station. The fastest and cheapest way to move to and from Narita Airport is by train. Take the Japan Railways Narita line to Chiba Station (¥300), then transfer to the Sobu rapid service to Tokyo station (¥700). Another option is to catch the Keisei Limited Express to Ueno Park (¥700), where you can connect with the subway system.

UNIQUELY TOKYO

It is said that in order to understand the Japanese you must bathe with them. They have made an art form of bathing, and a visit to a traditional public bath house can be an eye-opening experience. (Do be careful not to confuse bath houses with the entirely different experience of sopurando, or "soap-lands.") These single-sex, communal bathhouses, known as **sento**, are places that men go to relax with the guys, and women with the women.

The first difference between western and Japanese baths is the purpose: the goal is to soak, gossip, and tell jokes, not to get clean. In fact, you must scrupulously clean yourself with soap and water while sitting on a stool outside the bath before you climb in. Bathers sometimes wash each other's backs and rinse each other off. Avoid getting soap into the bath itself.

Once inside the bath, you may find the Japanese people suddenly daring; they may laugh, gesture, make surprisingly blunt comments or ask very personal questions. Remember that you can and should joke and query right back. Smile, have fun, don't take anything too seriously, and you are likely to leave the bath relaxed, with a whole new perspective on the Japanese.

You can find a sento in just about any residential neighborhood. Ask your innkeeper to point you towards a particularly good one. Most are fairly basic, but a few have themes (the "Jungle" sento, "Amusements" sento, etc.) **Sento Tsubameyu** [3-14-5 Ueno, Taitouku] is a good introduction to these Japanese baths. The sento is open from 6am to midnight, and is only closed on Monday. Consider arriving right at opening time, which is when the local morning bathers' association meets here.

Council Travel

Sanno Grand Building, Room 102
2-14-2 Nagata-Cho
Chiyoda-Ku, Tokyo 100 JAPAN
☎ (03) 3581 5517
Fax 03/ 3581 5519

Times to Call: 9:30am to 5:30pm
Type of Provider: Discount travel agent
Areas of Specialty: Worldwide

DESTINATIONS	SAMPLE ROUND TRIP FARE	STANDARD ECONOMY FARE
London	¥115,000	¥485,000
Los Angeles	¥90,000	¥294,000
New York	¥110,000	¥398,000
Sydney	¥120,000	¥335,500

In Business Since: 1947
Payment Methods: Cash, bank transfer

Open from 10am to 2pm Saturdays, for walk-in clients only. The Japanese branch of Council Travel does not handle intra-Asian flights.

(See the Council Travel listing in the Chicago chapter for company background.)

Jupiter Air of Japan

779-3 Azuma-Cho
Narita, Chiba 286 JAPAN
☎ (04) 76 24 21 57, (04) 76 42 48 79
Fax 04/ 76 24 24 58
Contact: Miss Hayashi

Times to Call: 9am to 5:30pm
Type of Provider: Courier company
Areas of Specialty: Worldwide

DESTINATIONS	SAMPLE ROUND TRIP FARE	STANDARD ECONOMY FARE	LENGTH OF STAY
London	¥120,000	¥485,000	up to 3 mos.

Payment Methods: Cash, bank transfer

Courier Duties on Return Trip: Yes
In Business Since: 1989
Recommended Advance Reservations: 0 to 3 months
Luggage: One carry-on only

All Jupiter flights from Tokyo are on hold until early 1995, when London flights may resume. When flights are running, they do keep a cancellation phone list. Jupiter strongly favors repeat business.

Linehaul Express

6th Floor M-Y Mita Building
5-29-17 Shiba
Minato-Ku, Tokyo 108 JAPAN
☎ (03) 37 69 83 54
Fax 03/ 37 69 94 58
Contact: Mr. Makino or Miss Abeh

Times to Call: 9:30am to 5:30pm
(Bilingual recording available after hours.)
Type of Provider: Courier company
Areas of Specialty: Worldwide

DESTINATIONS	SAMPLE ROUND TRIP FARE	STANDARD ECONOMY FARE	LENGTH OF STAY
Hong Kong	¥37,000	¥136,900	up to 10 days

Payment Methods: Cash, bank transfer
Courier Duties on Return Trip: Yes
Minimum Age: 18 years
In Business Since: 1989
Recommended Advance Reservations: 2 or 3 weeks

In high season the Hong Kong fare can run up to ¥60,000, which is still less than half of the lowest published fare.

In late 1994, Linehaul will introduce flights from Osaka to Hong Kong, with courier connections to London and Frankfurt.

STA Travel

4th Floor, Nukariya Building
1-16-20, Minami-Ikebukuro
Toshima-Ku, Tokyo 171 JAPAN
☎ (03) 5391 2922
Fax 03/ 5391 2923

Times to Call: 9am to 5pm
Type of Provider: Discount travel agency
Areas of Specialty: Worldwide

DESTINATIONS	SAMPLE ROUND TRIP FARE	STANDARD ECONOMY FARE
Bangkok	¥79,000	¥201,900
London	¥92,000	¥485,000
Los Angeles	¥66,000	¥294,000
New York	¥109,000	¥398,000
Paris	¥92,000	¥485,000

Payment Methods: Cash, money order, certified check, personal check, Visa, MasterCard, American Express
In Business Since: 1975

STA is the world's largest travel organization for students and young, independent travelers. They have 120 locations worldwide. Some of their best fares require student ID, or carry a maximum age.

Their tickets are highly flexible, usually good for one year and requiring no advance purchase. Date changes can be made at any office worldwide for $25; refunds cost only $50 to $75. Such flexible tickets are a wise choice for travelers going on long trips without fully concrete itineraries. STA tickets are priced based on one-way tickets, which makes it easy to book open-jaw flights.

Wholesale Courier

☎ (04) 76 92 03 11
Fax 04/ 76 92 03 09
Contact: Wai

Times to Call: 9am to 5pm, except closed for lunch 12pm to 1pm
Type of Provider: Courier company
Areas of Specialty: Asia

DESTINATIONS	SAMPLE ROUND TRIP FARE	STANDARD ECONOMY FARE	LENGTH OF STAY
Bangkok	¥40,000	¥201,900	up to 6 mos.
Hong Kong	¥35,000	¥136,900	up to 6 mos.
Singapore	¥45,000	¥217,300	up to 6 mos.

Payment Methods: Cash, bank transfer
Courier Duties on Return Trip: No
Minimum Age: 18 years
In Business Since: 1986
Recommended Advance Reservations: 3 months

These flights have gotten popular, so it is best to call a full three months in advance. If you cannot book far ahead, call to check on last-minute discounts, which can drop to ¥10,000. This company maintains a cancellation phone list for existing customers. All flights are on Northwest Airlines.

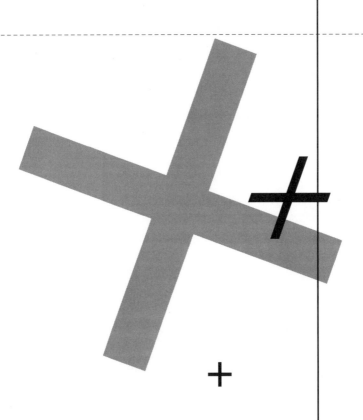

APPENDIXES

Air Pass Programs

If you plan to travel extensively in a large country or region, the air pass option is worth looking into. Air pass programs offer the convenience and speed of air travel at a price that can often be competitive with land-based transportation. When you factor in the value of your time, flying may offer a clearly superior alternative.

A few air pass programs operate just like Eurail tickets, good for unlimited travel during a certain period of time. Typically, however, these programs offer the traveler a booklet of coupons, where each coupon is valid for one flight segment. In some cases, the passes are valid for travel anywhere an airline flies in a particular country, as in the case of American Airlines' Visit USA pass. In other cases, several airlines cooperate to offer a program which covers several countries in a region. For example, the Euroflyer Pass offers flights throughout Europe, courtesy of an agreement between Sabena, Air Inter, CSA, and Air France.

These programs usually require that you purchase your air pass before you arrive in the region; American Airlines' Visit USA pass, for example, cannot be purchased in the United States. Note that many air passes can be used by citizens of the country being visited, as long as the passes themselves are purchased abroad. Furthermore, some programs restrict air pass sales to travelers who purchased their international ticket on the sponsoring airline.

It is wise to ask whether flights that connect through a non-destination airport require only one coupon (as they should), or two coupons (as they sometimes do). This is especially true with passes which cover several countries. If to fly from Rome to Zurich you must use two coupons and fly through Amsterdam, using an air pass may be a poor investment of both time and money.

In general, airlines price these passes differently, depending on the departure point of the traveler's international ticket. There are typically three price levels: passes are cheapest when purchased in the Third World, more expensive when purchased in Europe, and most expensive when purchased in Japan.

Some programs allow you to buy exactly the number of coupons you need, while others have a minimum and/or a maximum. Most companies will allow you to return unused coupons for a refund, but check with individual airlines before you make your purchase.

Telephone numbers provided are the direct, toll-free air pass hotlines for each airline's United States operations. Elsewhere in the world, call the main telephone number for the appropriate airline in your country. Unless otherwise specified, prices are listed in U.S. dollars.

AFRICA

Royal Air Moroc, ☎ (800) 344 6726
Discover Morocco

This simple air pass program offers travelers four coupons for $149, or six coupons for $169. All coupons must be used within six months of the first flight.

South African Airways, ☎ (800) 722 9675
Africa Explorer

This rather restrictive and finicky program prices each flight segment differently. Travelers can buy a minimum of four and a maximum of eight coupons, which must be used within 30 days. You must purchase an international flight on any airline in order to qualify. There is a 25 percent cancellation charge. The price quoted on a sample itinerary of Johannesburg – Cape Town – Port Elizabeth – Durban – Johannesburg was $320. To add on a flight from Johannesburg to Nairobi, Kenya and back costs an additional $541.

ASIA

Air India, ☎ (800) 223 7776
Discover India

This program operates in conjunction with Indian Air, and offers unlimited flights during a 21-day period for $400. The period starts the day of your first domestic flight. Travelers may not revisit a city except in order to make a flight connection.

Visit Indonesia

These coupons run $100 apiece. You can buy anywhere from three to ten coupons, and must use all of them within 60 days. Flights must start in Bali, Djakarta or Medan. You use one ticket per destination, regardless of the number of connections required.

Thai Airways International, ☎ (800) 426 5204

Discover Thailand

This pass must be purchased in the United States. It offers four flight coupons for $239, with up to four additional coupons for $50 each. All coupons must be used within 60 days of the first flight. You must confirm the date and destination of your first flight, and set your itinerary (with open dates) in advance.

AUSTRALIA

Ansett Airlines, ☎ (800) 366 1300

Visit Australia Pass

Pass must be purchased before arrival in Australia, in conjunction with an international flight. Additional coupons can be purchased once in Australia at any Ansett or EastWest ticketing location. Not available in Japan. In North America, you can buy a minimum of four coupons, and a maximum of eight coupons per pass. Outside North America, the minimum is only two coupons. Round trip, circle trip, and open jaw flights are permitted. The Exclusive Pass (excluding Western Australia cities) costs AU$640 for four coupons, AU$160 for each additional coupon. The Inclusive Pass (includes all Australian cities) runs AU$740 for four coupons, AU$210 for each additional coupon.

Qantas Airlines, ☎ (800) 227 4500

Australia Explorer Pass

Much like Ansett's pass, this program has different price structures depending on zone in which the pass holder seeks to travel. Dates and destinations can be left open. Purchase the pass in conjunction with an international ticket from anywhere in the Western

Hemisphere. The minimum book of four coupons costs $440, or $554 including flights to Perth, Ayers Rock, Alice Springs or the outer islands. Additional coupons cost $121 each (or $146 for the outlying destinations). Travelers may purchase up to eight coupons, and the last four coupons can be bought in Australia. You can reserve seats ahead of time, or just show up at the airport and take your chances.

EUROPE

Air France, ☎ (800) 237 2747
Euroflyer Pass

This pass is a result of a cooperative deal between Air France, Air Inter, CSA, and Sabena. Coupons cost $120 each, and are valid for any European flight on any of the partner airlines. The pass has a seven day minimum, and a 60-day maximum. To qualify, you must purchase the pass in conjunction with a USA to Paris ticket. You may purchase anywhere from three to nine coupons.

British Airways, ☎ (800) 247 9297
Europe Air Pass

Minimum of three coupons and used over at least seven days, with no maximums. All flights are on British Airways, Air Gibraltar, TAT (France) or Deutsche BA. Pass must start or end in the UK. Each direct flight costs $75, $98, $120 or $150, depending on the length of the flight. If you change planes on a non-direct flight, it costs two coupons. You must pay for your trans-Atlantic flight, which means that frequent flier flights do not qualify. Cities served include Ankara, Berlin, Casablanca, Gibraltar, London, Lyon, Moscow, Paris, Prague, and Stuttgart. You must reserve and pay for your pass seven days in advance of your first flight.

Iberia Airlines, ☎ (800) 772 4642
Visit Spain

This pass lets you fly in a circuit around Spain, without returning to any city more than once. You must start and stop the circuit in the same city. The minimum of four coupons costs $249, and each additional coupon costs $50. You must purchase your trans-Atlantic flight, rather than using frequent flier miles, in order to qualify. You need not fly to Europe on Iberia. A surcharge of $50 applies if you fly to the Canary Islands. All travel must be completed within 60 days. There is additional $50 surcharge for travel between June 15 and September 30.

Scandinavian Airlines (SAS), ☎ (800) 221 2350
Visit Scandinavia Pass

This pass covers flights anywhere SAS flies in Denmark, Norway, and Sweden. The first two segments cost $80, the next two cost $70, and the last two cost $60. You can purchase a minimum of one and a maximum of six coupons. You must choose your destinations in advance. Dates can be changed at no charge, but changing destinations will cost you $50.

LATIN AMERICA

Aero Peru, ☎ (800) 777 7717
Visit South America

Aero Peru's pass is a package deal, which includes a round trip flight from the United States to Lima. Prices increase during the high season, from July 1 to August 15. From Miami you get a round trip to Lima plus six South American flights for $999, or $1,184 in high season. From Los Angeles it's $1,396 or $1,580. All South American flights go through Lima, so you really get a flight to Lima plus the opportunity to visit three of the following countries: Argentina, Bolivia, Brazil, Chile, Colombia, or Ecuador. The exception of the Lima rule is that the flight from Santiago to Buenos Aires is direct. Extra segments cost $100 each. All flights must be completed within 45 days.

Mexicana Airlines, ☎ (800) 531 7921
Discover Mexico

Prices are lower than regular excursion fares, but not as good as the lowest discounted fares. Prices are determined by the city pairs involved. International travel on Aeromexico or Mexicana is required. Travelers must purchase a minimum of three coupons, two of which can be international segments. Sample itinerary: San Francisco–Mexico City–Cancun–Mazatlan–Mexico City–San Francisco for

$1,038. You must stay a minimum of two days, and a maximum of 45. Tickets become non-refundable after commencement of travel.

NORTH AMERICA

AirBC, ☎ (800) 456 5717
AirPass

Regional airline AirBC offers California residents traveling in Western Canada passes for unlimited standby flights. AirBC flights from Portland and Seattle to Vancouver are also included). The price is $329 for one week's unlimited travel, or $439 for two weeks. The pass must be purchased in California. AirBC's territory covers British Columbia, Alberta, Saskatchewan, and Manitoba.

American Airlines, ☎ (800) 433 7300
Visit USA Pass

This pass is only sold in conjunction with a trans-Atlantic fare bought in a foreign country. Travelers can buy between three and 14 coupons. The price is $549 for a booklet of three coupons, and then $100 for each additional coupon. A 24-hour advance reservation is required for each flight. Travelers should purchase this pass when they buy their international ticket.

America West Airlines, ☎ (800) 235 9292
Visit USA

Tickets must be purchased before arrival in the United States, and are non-refundable, non-endorsable, and valid only on America West. Reservations are permitted, as is flying standby. You must decide which cities you want to visit in advance, and confirm your first flight. The rest can be left open, but you are better off reserving all of your flights, and changing them later if necessary. There are actually two programs here: the System Program gives you a minimum of four flights (maximum of 12) within the continental U.S. for $319. Cities served include New York, Washington D.C., Orlando, Chicago, San Francisco, Los Angeles, among others. The Tri-State program starts at $139 for a minimum of 2 coupons, valid only in California, Nevada and Arizona. Add-on coupons to Mexico City and the Grand Canyon are available for enrollees in either program. The fine print reads "To be eligible for this program, applicants must reside at least 100 miles beyond any U.S. border in a country or commonwealth territory other than the 50 United States and the District of Colombia, and arrive via the scheduled services of any air carrier." Travelers originating in Asia or Australia should contact their local America West office, or the agent issuing the international tickets in order to get the specific fare on these passes. Many longer flights connect through Phoenix or Las Vegas; if you must change planes there, it will cost you two coupons, so try to book direct flights.

Canadian Airlines International, ☎ (800) 426 7000
Visit USA Fares

Rather than coupons, CAI's program offers special discounts on domestic flights. Travelers need a trans-oceanic ticket in order to qualify for the discounts. Prices are different for each city pair, and are often higher than the lowest APEX fares. Nonetheless, this may be a good bet for last-minute, long haul flights.

Continental Airlines, ☎ (800) 435 0040
Visit USA Fare

This pass allows you to purchase between three and ten coupons, for between $309 and $659. Dates may remain open but complete routing must be specified. Ticket must be issued in conjunction with an international ticket. Coupons expire after 60 days. Except at Denver, Houston, and Newark, changing planes at a connecting airport counts as a stopover and requires an additional coupon. Reservations must be confirmed before commencement of each flight. This is the cheapest standard air pass in the USA, but it can be hard to find space on the most popular flights during peak season.

Delta Air Lines, ☎ (800) 241 4141
Standby Travel Pass

Possibly the best deal in North America, this pass allows unlimited air travel anywhere in the continental USA, assuming that there is an empty seat on the plane. No reservations are accepted. Nationality does not matter, but you must "permanently" reside outside the Western Hemisphere in order to qualify. (Americans studying abroad do not qualify, but those working abroad do.) The pass must be bought in conjunction with a round trip ticket originating outside the USA. Once you have the pass, call the toll-free number listed above for advice on your chances of getting on a particular flight. Early morning and late evening flights are usually the least full. If the flight looks full, get to the airport early, and be the first Standby Pass holder on the waiting list. The 30-day pass costs $549, and the 60-day pass is $899.

Hawaiian Airlines, ☎ (800) 367 5320
Hawaiian Air Pass

Under this program pass holders can take an unlimited number of flights anywhere in the state of Hawaii for the duration of the pass. All flights must be reserved in advance, even if only moments in advance from an airport telephone. Hawaiians can buy this pass, if they do it in conjunction with a flight to and from the mainland. Prices are as follows: five days for $169, seven days for $189, ten days for $229, and fourteen days for $269.

Kiwi International Airlines, ☎ (800) 538 5494
Kiwi Bonus Pack

The pack includes six coupons good for one-way flights to or from the Newark hub and Atlanta, Chicago, and Orlando. Tickets are valid for one full year from date of first flight. The Bonus Pack costs $590, or $98 per segment.

Northwest Airlines, (call your travel agent outside the USA).
See America Pass

Travelers must purchase this pass abroad, and in fact will find Northwest agents in the United States quite unwilling to divulge information on this program. Prices are lowest if you purchase the pass in conjunction with an international flight on Northwest. Also, prices increase a bit for summer and holiday periods. You may buy between three and ten coupons, which in low season will cost you a total of $349 to $709. You must determine your routing in advance, but you can leave the dates open. Passes expire 60 days after the first coupon is used, or 120 days after arrival in the USA, whichever comes first. Only two stopovers are permitted at any one point, and only two round trip transcontinental flights without enroute stopovers are permitted.

Who Says Standby Flights are Dead?

Years ago, you could walk up to the airport ticket counter minutes before departure, and if empty seats remained, you could fly at the very low "standby" price. Then someone from the airlines realized that they could probably make more money by forcing last-minute travelers to pay a premium, and the standby flight nearly disappeared.

I say nearly, because standby fares can still be found, if you know where to look. The airlines no longer sell standbys, but certain discount travel agencies still do. The logic is this: You buy a standby ticket for a certain date, at a very good price. The airline continues to try to sell your seat. If someone comes to the airport 15 minutes before departure, he will have to pay the airline's premium, but he will get your seat. If they still have empty seats at departure time, then you are allowed to board, and the airline has gained some revenue.

It is a win-win situation, as long as you have a backup plan in case you don't get onto the plane. If the next flight is in a few hours, this is probably a good deal. If you live near the airport, and it won't be a huge inconvenience for you to return to the airport another day, it is still a good deal. But if it will cause you great emotional pain to miss the flight, pay the extra money for a confirmed seat.

Another time to use standby fares is when all of the discounted seats on a flight are sold out. Chances are good that some of the higher priced seats will remain open, and standby passengers will be allowed to fill those seats. But by their very nature, standby flights are not a sure thing. If your plans are flexible enough, here are some discount agencies that deal in standby fares.

Air-Tech Ltd. (New York)
☎ (212) 219 7000

Air-Tech specializes in region-to-region travel. Most of their flights connect San Francisco, Los Angeles, and New York with major Western European cities, and with Mexico. You purchase a Flightpass voucher from them, which you exchange for a boarding pass at the airport, if space is available on the flight. You must be flexible in both destination and date of travel. They ask you to list three major cities which would be acceptable as destinations, and to provide a "travel window" of acceptable departure dates. A few days before your window starts, you call to find out which flights offer you the best odds. You may end up flying to Amsterdam on Wednesday, instead of London on Tuesday. If this kind of system works for you, give them a call. Summer one-way prices were $169 from the East Coast, or $269 from California.

Discount Travel International
☎ (800) FLY 4 DTI

DTI is constantly foraging for new bargains, so you should call them to get the latest information. In general, they book standby seats on the low-fare airlines for flights withing the USA, and also book flights on some of the most popular international routes. Flights typically depart from most major U.S. airports. DTI also sells discounted confirmed seats on most of the same flights. Sample fare: one-way New York to Miami for $125 standby, or $149 confirmed.

Four Winds Travel (New York)
☎ (212) 777 7637

Call for information on domestic standby flights.

Now Voyager (New York)
☎ (718) 656 5000

Now Voyager offers a wide variety of coast-to-coast standbys, as well as occasional international bargains.

Piece of Mind Travel (San Francisco)
☎ (415) 864 1995

This is San Francisco's only standby broker so far. They sell both domestic and European space-available tickets.

Tower Air
☎ (800) 34 TOWER

Tower is the only airline we know of which openly offers discounted standby fares at the gate. For example, their already cheap $149

Standby
Flights

coast-to-coast flights go for $119 on a standby basis.

Way to Go Travel (Los Angeles)
☎ (213) 466 1126

Way to Go has some great deals on both domestic and international standbys. Sample: New York to Kingston, Jamaica for $313 round trip.

Get "Bumped" and Fly Free Next Time

Across the country, thousands of air travelers are voluntarily giving up their confirmed seats on oversold flights. Why, you ask? Because the airlines make it worthwhile.

Airlines regularly sell more tickets than there are seats on the plane. The purpose of this "overbooking" is to make up for the estimated 10 percent of customers who fail to show up for a scheduled flight.

When flights are overbooked, airlines would rather leave volunteers behind than force people to miss flights. When the airlines need to "bump" someone from a flight, they offer incentives to encourage people to volunteer.

If you get bumped, you get priority for the next available flight. Also, you usually get a free round trip flight to be used at a later date. Often you get free meals and a free hotel room, too.

If your schedule allows it, there are ways of increasing your chance of being bumped and getting a free flight.

Reserve a seat on a popular flight. Find out which flights are busiest. To avoid suspicion you might say, "I have a friend who is also interested in that flight. How does it look for her?" If you must arrive somewhere on a specific day, make sure there is a flight with available seating following the one from which you hope to be bumped. This way, if you are lucky enough to get bumped, you can still arrive that same day.

If you are completely flexible about when you fly, put yourself on the waiting list of several busy flights. That way, if you do get a confirmed seat on one, you'll know it's full, and you will have vastly improved your chance of getting bumped.

Travel when the airlines are the busiest. Try Thanksgiving, Christmas, and other holidays. Wednesday, Friday, and Sunday are the busiest days of the week. Early morning departures and early evening arrivals are the most popular flights.

Arrive at the airport early. When you check in, ask if the flight is full. Volunteer to get bumped as soon as you have a boarding pass, before the airline announces that the flight is overbooked. Get your name near the top of the waiting list; if you wait until just before takeoff, there will be a teeming hoard of volunteers ahead of you.

Sometimes the airlines engage in "bidding for bumpees." At first they offer something small, such as a $50 coupon towards a future flight. If enough people voluntarily give up their seats for $50 each, the airlines save a lot of money. If they still need to vacate some seats, they may up the offer to a one-way transcontinental flight. Be aware of their little bidding game, and hang in there as long as it seems advantageous. I look for a free round trip ticket any time I save an airline's reputation for service by giving up my seat.

Packing Light

To some it may seem to go against the grain of capitalist society, but when traveling, LESS IS MORE! The less gear you schlep around, the happier you will be.

Those taking courier flights are usually compelled to pack light. But all of us would do well to travel as light as couriers do. Buy a good backpack, and make sure it is small enough to fit on the plane. Ideally the bag should have multiple compartments, and should convert from a backpack to a suitcase at the pull of a zipper. [A good example is the Maximum Legal Carry-On, by Patagonia, ☎ (800) 336 9090.]

What to pack? Everyone has slightly different needs, but the typical vacation traveler will rarely need more than the following for a two week trip:

> **1** lightweight jacket
> **1** rain poncho
> **1** sweater or sweatshirt
> **3** shirts or blouses
> **1-2** pairs of pants or skirts
> **1-2** pairs of shorts
> **3** pairs of socks
> **4** changes of underwear
> **1** bathing suit
> **1** hat
> **1** pair of decent walking shoes
> **1** pair of beach/shower sandals
> **1** fairly nice outfit
> Toiletries
> Medicine
> Contraceptives
> Sun glasses
> The smallest towel you can stand
> Camera and film
> Pen light
> Multi-function knife
> Address book
> Travel alarm clock

Plastic bags for dirty laundry, etc.
Small day pack
Small, durable water bottle
Luggage locks
Maps and guidebooks
Pictures and postcards of home, to show new friends
Documents, tickets, money, and a moneybelt to hold it all

Start with enough toiletries for only two weeks. Buy or borrow more as you go along. Bring a tube of liquid laundry detergent, and plan to wash a few items in your hotel sink every couple of days. Keep in mind that dark colors hide the dirt. Bring clothes that fit one or two color schemes, so you can wear anything with anything else. Avoid clothes that wrinkle easily. If you will be hostelling, bring a hostel sleep sack instead of renting one each night.

Traveling businessmen can usually get away with one dark suit, an extra pair of pants, three shirts and several ties (assuming frequent visits to the dry cleaners). The key is to foster the appearance of variety for the people you meet, not for yourself. If you are on a solo business trip and you will be seeing different clients each day, they'll never know what you wore yesterday.

Zip up your pack, put it on, and step outside. If you can't easily walk 10 blocks with it on, go back and unpack some of those things you thought you "might" need. If you really need them, you can buy them there. Remember, there is a reason that experienced travelers pack light. They know they will be happier and more mobile than if they didn't.

Courier Adventures

Courier travel is so easy—it amazes me that more people do not take advantage of it. Your duties are simple and unburdensome, yet your airfare is half that of other passengers. And if you are a seasoned traveler, you probably already pack light and bring carry-on luggage only.

To illustrate how easy it is to fly as a courier, let me walk you through a courier flight that I took recently from New York to London.

The first step was to plan my date ranges. The more flexible you are, the easier it is to fly cheap. I decided to stay for about two weeks, and to depart between March 17 and March 19.

I would have preferred to fly from California to London, but by the time I called the courier companies, all of the flights from the West Coast to London were booked. Not easily deterred by such minor details, I started calling the New York courier companies. (New York is, after all, on the way.) Sure enough, I found a flight as a courier for Halbart Express, one of the world's biggest courier companies. The dates were perfect, so I booked the flight by telephone.

Next, I used some frequent flier miles (earned on a previous courier trip; I've also used American Express student tickets to fly across the United States cheaply) to get a free flight from San Francisco to New York. That meant that the total cost for the flight from California to London was only $239. Not a bad deal!

I got into New York the night before my Halbart courier flight, and spent the evening enjoying the Friday night bustle in the East Village. I had called Halbart to reconfirm my flight, and was given very simple instructions: "Meet the Halbart representative at the American Eagle counter at JFK Airport at 2pm."

A friend dropped me off at the airport a bit before 2pm the next day. We noticed a Halbart truck parked outside the American Eagle counter. "Good sign," I thought. Inside, I saw a man with a Halbart jacket and a Halbart cap. "This is too easy," I said to myself.

I walked up and said, "Hi. I'm the courier for London." He handed me my round trip ticket, and three pages of written courier instructions. On the flight out, I would be stopping in Boston, where the mailbags would actually be loaded onto the plane. On the flight home, I would go directly from London to New York. Each page of the instructions corresponded to one leg of the round trip. I asked the Halbart representative to wait while I read through the brief instructions. The Halbart man verified that I was accompanying mailbags on the Boston-London leg only. I was to call Halbart's London affiliate upon my arrival, to ask if there was anything further to be done. I was also instructed to call two business days before my return flight, to request instructions.

The Halbart rep left, and I headed for my flight. In Boston, I arrived early at the designated meeting place, under the large London banner at the American Airlines counter. A few minutes after the listed meeting time, the Boston Halbart rep arrived, toting two large orange plastic mail sacks. He checked me in, wished me a safe trip, and pointed me towards the gate.

The flight was easy, and really no different from any other flight. I arrived in London early in the morning, and promptly called the local Halbart office. I said, "Hello, I'm the courier from Boston, and I've just arrived." He said, "That's all, you may go, sir." I didn't have to do a thing, and I was now officially on vacation.

At the end of my trip, I called Halbart's London affiliate for instructions. It turned out that they had nothing for me to accompany. I did very little to earn my discounted airfare on the way to London, but I did absolutely nothing on my return flight. I was just another passenger.

Too easy.

INSIDER REPORT:

Review of Jupiter Air's Los Angeles-Singapore Run

Researcher Byron B. Deeter agreed to review the courier operation of Jupiter Air on a recent flight to Singapore. The following is his report.

My motivation for deciding to try courier travel was simple: money. I didn't have a lot of it. My girlfriend was spending the summer working in Singapore, and although I wanted to visit her, I could not afford to pay the fares that the airlines were asking. Three months in advance the cheapest conventional flight I could find was around $1,500 round trip. When I found a courier flight on United Airlines for $550 round trip, on the dates I wanted to fly, the decision was easy. Three months later I was landing at Los Angeles International Airport (LAX), about to meet my contact from the courier company and begin my trip. The arrangements at LAX were surprisingly easy.

Along with one other courier, I met the contact at our pre-determined location two hours before my scheduled take-off. At that point our contact called the main Los Angeles office on his cellular phone to let them know that we had been found, and that everything was a go. He then helped us check in, as some of those full-fare people do, at the first-class counter. Mind you, they were not about to let me fly first class, but because of their relationship with the airlines, we were able to check in that way. This enabled us to bypass the long coach-class check-in lines, and essentially walk right up to the counter.

At this point potential couriers will want to take note of three things: I was able to check in a suitcase, they did not give me my return ticket to the USA at that time, and on this leg of the trip I was unable to get frequent flier miles. Different companies handle these matters in different ways. As for the luggage, I got lucky. Often times couriers are allowed only a single carry-on bag, since the courier company is using your checked baggage allotment. But I was allowed one carry-on, and up to two checked bags. Additionally, I never touched the mailbags, nor did I have to carry a document pouch with shipping manifests. Jupiter Air's agreement with United Airlines is such that they simply have to show United that someone is sitting in a seat on the plane in order for the shipment to be considered properly escorted. I didn't even need to hold on to the claim checks for the mailbags.

Essentially, with the ticket in my name, I flew as a normal passenger. I say essentially, because there were the two other exceptions I mentioned above. First, Jupiter Air gave me only a photocopy of my return ticket on United Airlines, and it had "OPEN" marked for the date. They said that the return ticket would be sent over with another courier to protect their interests. This made me slightly nervous, but made sense, as their main objective was to ensure that their freight gets shipped. This way, if I do not show up at the Singapore airport to accompany mailbags on the return trip, they can use the ticket for

221

another courier. The photocopy of the return ticket is to appease immigration officials by showing that you do indeed intend to return. Second, the ticket had marked on it "NO MILES," which in airline-worker-lingo means "laugh at this kid when he tries to get frequent flier mileage on top of the great deal he already has." Again, this varies with the company you travel with, and its agreement with the airline.

Frankly, I was amazed at how easy it had been! I had literally spent months in anticipation of this trip. I had booked my flight three months in advance. Then all of a sudden, I was in Singapore like every other traveler on that flight. People had paid three to four times as much, for a seat right next to mine! The ease of my flight was also increased by the fact that the plane was far under capacity, so I was able to stretch out across four empty seats and sleep for much of the flight.

However, this account would not be truly informative if I were not to relate a negative as well. After a fabulous week-long stay in Singapore, I arrived at the airport on a Sunday morning to meet my contact, get my ticket, and fly home to California. I had called Jupiter Air's local contact number earlier in the week, and was told everything was in good shape. I was told to meet their representative at a set place, one hour and fifteen minutes before my flight was set to depart. Take note of the tight time frame—I didn't until it was too late. I arrived at the meeting point, two other couriers arrived, and then the Jupiter rep arrived.

The problem was that there were THREE of us, and TWO tickets in his hand. It was not standard procedure for couriers to duel over the tickets. The rep had simply forgotten one ticket at the office—mine. It was now just over one hour before my flight was to depart, I had no ticket, and his office was half an hour away. Even if he could have gotten there and back in time, he was just a delivery boy, and did not have the key to get in.

Although the delivery boy knew nothing, he did have contact phone numbers, and I immediately placed a call to their downtown office. I think that being genuinely angry, and the fact that I aggressively asserted myself at this point made a large difference. I would suggest doing the same if ever faced with a similar situation.

I flatly demanded that the Jupiter official get out of bed and come down the airport himself. Although I missed my scheduled flight, he was able to get me on a flight to LAX that departed only 30 minutes later, passing through a different layover city.

To Jupiter Air's credit, they admitted that they had made a mistake, and they eventually solved the problem. On the whole I would have to say that the experience was a positive one, and I look forward to flying as a courier again in the future. The mix-up at Jupiter's Singapore office added unneeded stress to my return, but it was adequately handled. As a bonus, because of the hurried conditions under which my return ticket was issued, they neglected to mark it "NO MILES," so I was able to get frequent flier credit. Best of all, I was able to travel to a place I would not have been able to afford to visit otherwise, and I had a great time doing it.

Best of luck in your own travels! Bon Voyage!

"Joe Can't Make It; Welcome to Japan"

Steve Rubenstein is a columnist for the San Francisco Chronicle. In this two-part column, Steve recounts his Singapore courier experience, which was booked at the last minute, and included a stopover in Japan.

They sent me to the other side of the world last week. I was to meet the man in the black windbreaker.

Someone had to do it. Someone trustworthy. They sent me anyway.

The mission was to go to Tokyo and Singapore, and hand a slip of paper to a man in a black windbreaker. This is the job of the international air courier. A courier flies around the world on a moment's notice. On the other side of the world, the courier hands over his baggage claim check.

"Think you can do that?" said the courier dispatcher.

Yes. I do. I went to college.

"Good," she said. "Then we're sending you to Tokyo and Singapore. You leave the day after tomorrow."

Couriers are the latest fuzzy gray area in international travel.

223

Overnight mail companies recruit couriers to carry sacks of express mail as baggage, because passenger baggage clears customs faster than unaccompanied cargo. The actual courier, who pays nothing or next to nothing to fly around the world, is something of a technicality. The courier carries nothing himself, and never touches the mail sacks.

"You just sit on the plane," she said.

The courier nodded. Being a newspaperman in his other life, he knows how to sit around, doing nothing.

Before departure at the airport came the final briefing from the head courier.

"When you get to Tokyo, you are to meet a man in a black windbreaker. His name is Joe. He'll be at the No. 1 customs counter. Give him this claim check."

The sack of express mail had already been checked onto the plane. What was inside the sack? the courier asked.

"You don't need to know." said the head courier. "Contracts, documents, boring stuff. A lot of paperwork."

Stick to the basics, he said. Fly around the world, meet Joe. Give him the scrap of paper.

The courier got on the plane. A flight attendant traipsed over and handed him a hot washcloth. Shortly after takeoff, the courier got another one. Singapore Airlines is big on hot washcloths. This was a seven-washcloth flight.

Forty thousand feet over the Pacific, today became tomorrow. An entire Sunday vanished. Anything can happen on a cloak-and-dagger mission to the other side of the world.

You'll get your day back later, said the sweet Singapore girl. Matter cannot be created nor destroyed. Don't worry. Have a washcloth.

And then the crescent moon and the other side of the world rose to meet the descending wheels of the flying machine.

This was Tokyo. Outside was a city of 18 million people. With any luck, one of them would be wearing a black windbreaker. There he was, inside the customs hall, at Counter No. 1.

"Joe?"

It wasn't Joe. Joe couldn't make it, he said. The courier had flown around the world to meet Joe, and Joe wasn't there.

The guy in the windbreaker said his name was Endo. The courier handed him the claim check.

"It's OK," he said. "I don't need the claim check. You can keep it."

Wait a minute, windbreaker man. The courier flew halfway around the world to give you a claim check, and now you don't want it?

"They know me here," he said. "I already picked up the sack. Welcome to Japan."

Tomorrow: On to Singapore!

Part 2: "$88 Cantaloupes And Keen-Eyed Cops"

In yesterday's column, I flew halfway around the world to meet a man in a black windbreaker.

I was an international air courier. It's legal, probably.

Express mail companies send overnight mail as passenger baggage, so it can clear customs quickly. The courier does nothing but sit on the plane and fly practically for free." Being a newspaperman, this courier new how to do nothing.

After meeting the man in the windbreaker, the courier had two days to spend in Tokyo. Spending two days in Tokyo means spending. Sticker shock hits the moment one enters a Tokyo supermarket, looking for a snack.

Cantaloupes were $88 each. This is not a misprint.

The courier did not have a cantaloupe. Instead, the courier went down the street to the mausoleum and checked in for the night.

Mausoleum hotels are all over downtown Tokyo. Each customer gets a plastic compartment, the size of a large coffin, stacked into the wall. The courier slept only inches from the coffin to the right (which snored) and the coffin to the left (which coughed) and the coffin overhead (whose corporeal occupant arose in its kimono every few minutes to go to the bathroom).

A mausoleum hotel is not quite the same as a mausoleum. In the morning, occupants get to wake up.

The courier crawled from his coffin, drank a pot of boring beverage called tea and did the museum and rock garden circuit. In Tokyo, you walk sideways, because everything is narrow, and you walk fast, because everyone else knows where he is going. No one steals in Tokyo; there are too many eye witnesses.

Before long it was time to head for the airport and meet another man in a black windbreaker.

"You courier?" he asked.

The courier bowed, this being Japan. The windbreaker man bowed back, jotted something on his clipboard, and melted into the night. High intrigue in foreign capitols.

By the time Singapore rolled to a stop outside the plane window, it was 2am and there was no one in a black windbreaker to claim the mailbag. Round and round it went on the baggage carrousel, the precious cargo of express mail.

"It's OK," said the customs man. "Nobody meets the 2am plane. They went to sleep. They'll get it later. Welcome to Singapore."

Singapore is a town that does not mess around. Singapore is an air-conditioned string of high rises and shopping malls—climatized, sanitized, Westernized—with orchids in the trees and condensation on the windows. Exotic Singapore looks much like exotic Houston.

Singapore has many rules, enforced by keen-eyed cops on every corner. No chewing gum ($200 fine), no feeding birds ($200 fine), no failing to flush toilets ($200 fine), no spitting ($200 fine), no littering ($1,000 fine) no drug trafficking (death, or 15 lashes of the whip, whichever is greater).

Before the day was out, the courier had smelled many orchids, passed through two museum and rung up four grand in unofficial fines. As the sun slipped into the Strait of Malacca, it was time to grab a cab for the airport and head home, before the cops could pick up the scent.

There was no time to snatch souvenirs. There was barely time to snatch back his missing day.

It's the International Date Line thing, the courier realized, as the plane shuttled between hemispheres. The courier had traded a perfectly good Sunday on the Westward journey in exchange for two consecutive Thursdays on the Eastward journey. It's a singular transaction, like $88 for a cantaloupe.

City	Country	City	Country
Abu Dhabi	United Arab Emirates	**P**apeete	Tahiti
Agadir	Morocco	Paris	France
Amsterdam	Netherlands	Philadelphia	USA
Athens	Greece	Port Louis	Mauritius
Auckland	New Zealand	Prague	Czech Republic
Bahrain	Bahrain	Puerto Vallarta	Mexico
Bali	Indonesia	**Q**uito	Ecuador
Bangkok	Thailand	**R**io de Janeiro	Brazil
Barcelona	Spain	Rome	Italy
Berlin	Germany	**S**an Francisco	USA
Bogota	Colombia	San Jose	Costa Rica
Bombay	India	San Juan	Puerto Rico (USA)
Boston	USA	San Salvador	El Salvador
Brussels	Belgium	Santiago	Chile
Budapest	Hungary	Santo Domingo	Dominican Republic
Buenos Aires	Argentina	Sao Paulo	Brazil
Cairo	Egypt	Seattle	USA
Cancun	Mexico	Seoul	South Korea
Caracas	Venezuela	Singapore	Singapore
Chicago	USA	Stockholm	Sweden
Copenhagen	Denmark	Sydney	Australia
Crete	Greece	**T**aipei	Taiwan
Dakar	Senegal	Tel Aviv	Israel
Delhi	India	Tokyo	Japan
Djakarta	Indonesia	Toronto	Canada
Dubai	United Arab Emirates	Toulouse	France
Dusseldorf	Germany	**V**ancouver	Canada
Frankfurt	Germany	**Z**urich	Switzerland
Gaborone	Botswana		
Guatemala City	Guatemala		
Guayaquil	Ecuador		
Hamburg	Germany		
Harare	Zimbabwe		
Ho Chi Minh City	Vietnam		
Hong Kong	Hong Kong		
Honolulu	USA		
Istanbul	Turkey		
Johannesburg	South Africa		
Kauai	USA		
Kingston	Jamaica		
Kuala Lumpur	Malaysia		
La Paz	Bolivia		
Lagos	Nigeria		
Larnaca	Cyprus		
Lima	Peru		
Lisbon	Portugal		
London	UK		
Los Angeles	USA		
Lusaka	Zambia		
Madrid	Spain		
Manchester	UK		
Manila	Philippines		
Maui	USA		
Melbourne	Australia		
Mendoza	Argentina		
Mexico City	Mexico		
Miami	USA		
Milan	Italy		
Montevideo	Uruguay		
Montreal	Canada		
Moscow	Russia		
Munich	Germany		
Nairobi	Kenya		
Nassau	Bahamas		
New York	USA		
Nice	France		
Orlando	USA		

Country	City
Argentina	Buenos Aires
	Mendoza
Australia	Melbourne
	Sydney
Bahamas	Nassau
Bahrain	Bahrain
Belgium	Brussels
Bolivia	La Paz
Botswana	Gaborone
Brazil	Rio de Janeiro
	Sao Paulo
Canada	Montreal
	Toronto
	Vancouver
Chile	Santiago
Colombia	Bogota
Costa Rica	San Jose
Cyprus	Larnaca
Czech Republic	Prague
Denmark	Copenhagen
Dominican Republic	Santo Domingo
Ecuador	Guayaquil
	Quito
Egypt	Cairo
El Salvador	San Salvador
France	Nice
	Paris
	Toulouse
Germany	Berlin
	Dusseldorf
	Frankfurt
	Hamburg
	Munich
Greece	Athens
	Crete
Guatemala	Guatemala City
Hong Kong	Hong Kong
Hungary	Budapest
India	Bombay
	Delhi
Indonesia	Bali
	Djakarta
Israel	Tel Aviv
Italy	Milan
	Rome
Jamaica	Kingston
Japan	Tokyo
Kenya	Nairobi
Malaysia	Kuala Lumpur
Mauritius	Port Louis
Mexico	Cancun
	Mexico City
	Puerto Vallarta
Morocco	Agadir
Netherlands	Amsterdam
New Zealand	Auckland
Nigeria	Lagos
Peru	Lima
Philippines	Manila
Portugal	Lisbon
Puerto Rico (USA)	San Juan
Russia	Moscow
Senegal	Dakar
Singapore	Singapore
South Africa	Johannesburg
South Korea	Seoul

Country	City
Spain	Barcelona
	Madrid
Sweden	Stockholm
Switzerland	Zurich
Tahiti	Papeete
Taiwan	Taipei
Thailand	Bangkok
Turkey	Istanbul
United Arab Emirates	Abu Dhabi
	Dubai
United Kingdom	London
	Manchester
Uruguay	Montevideo
USA	Boston
	Chicago
	Honolulu
	Kauai
	Los Angeles
	Maui
	Miami
	New York
	Orlando
	Philadelphia
	San Francisco
	Seattle
Venezuela	Caracas
Vietnam	Ho Chi Minh City
Zambia	Lusaka
Zimbabwe	Harare

229

Glossary of Terms

APEX / Acronym for "Advance Purchase Excursion" fare, which is typically the cheapest and most restricted fare you can buy directly from the airlines.

Around-the-world fares / A special class of consolidator ticket which typically involves using multiple airlines and stopovers to cheaply circumnavigate the globe, stopping to visit number of predetermined cities.

Bucket shop / Consolidators who sell tickets directly to the public.

Carry-on baggage / The allotment of luggage which you are allowed to bring on board the plane with you. On domestic U.S. flights, you can usually carry aboard one bag weighing less than 20 kilograms (44 pounds), and one bag small enough to fit under your seat. International flights may restrict you to a single carry-on bag. A carry-on limit of five kilograms could legally be enforced, but in reality this rarely happens on major international airlines. Often, those flying as couriers are only allowed to bring carry-on luggage.

Charter flights / The "Brand X" of the airline industry. Their distinct legal status makes it easy for them to alter routes as the seasons change. They run discounted flights to the most popular destinations at each time of year, often from major cities to sun or ski vacation spots.

Checked baggage / Luggage which is stored in the hold of the plane. On international flights, the limit is usually 20 kilograms (44 pounds). In the USA, the limit on domestic flights is two bags weighing a total of no more than 85 kilograms (140 pounds). Couriers typically must give up their checked baggage allotment in exchange for a discounted airfare.

Circle-Pacific fares / A special class of consolidator ticket which typically involves using multiple airlines and stopovers to fly around the Pacific Rim cheaply, stopping to visit number of predetermined cities.

Consolidator / The "factory outlet stores" of the airline industry. These agents buy excess seats from the airlines, and sell them at a steep discount. See also Bucket shop, Wholesaler.

Courier flight / A little-known mode of air travel in which passengers trade their checked baggage allotment to an international shipping company in exchange for a steeply discounted airfare on a major airline.

Ethnic specialty agency / Small, local bucket shops, usually run by and catering to members of a particular ethnic group.

Exporting tickets / The practice of selling air tickets by mail to third countries, to take advantage of particularly low airfares in some world markets. Most agents that can export tickets are in San Francisco and London. This practice is frowned on by the airlines, but (depending on the agent's agreement with the airline) not against any law.

High season / The time of year when passenger demand (and therefore airfares) are highest. Varies depending on the destination. Typically July and August in Europe and North America, January and February in Australia, and around Christmas in most of the Western world.

IATA / The International Air Transport Association, a cartel of international airlines which attempts to regulate the price of air travel.

Local currency strategy / A discount airfare trick that works when by exchanging money to a foreign currency and purchasing the ticket in that currency, the ticket is cheaper than buying the ticket in the currency of origin.

Low season / The time of year when few people seek to travel to a particular destination. Airline tickets are cheapest at this time.

One-way ticket / A ticket good only for travel from Point A to Point B. Known as a "single ticket" in the UK and Australia.

Onward ticket / A ticket valid for travel from Point A to Point B, and on to Point C. Often necessary at customs at Point B, as proof that you don't plan to stay illegally in their country.

Open-jaw ticket / A ticket which lets you fly into one city, spend your vacation traveling by land, and returning home from another city. For example, one might fly from the USA to London, travel by rail through Europe, and finally catch a flight in Athens to return to the

USA.

Return ticket / A ticket valid for travel from Point A to Point B, then returning back to Point A. Often necessary at customs at Point B, as proof that you don't plan to stay illegally in their country. Same as a round trip ticket.

Round trip / See Return ticket.

Scheduled flight / The legal status of flights on most major airlines. Provides more protection to the passenger in case of a cancelled or delayed flight.

Shoulder season / The period between high and low season, during which demand for air travel (and therefore cost of air travel) is moderate. Often the most cost-effective and least tourist-ridden time to travel.

Space-available fare / The modern equivalent of the old "standby fare." Passengers must purchase a space-available ticket at a special agency before arriving at the airport. Ten minutes before the flight, the ticket can be traded for a boarding pass if there are still empty seats on the plane.

Standby fare / Once the very cheap fare sold by airlines at the gate 10 minutes before departure. Now nearly non-existent. Last-minute tickets purchased from the airline at the gate are among the most expensive fares available.

Sufficient funds / An arbitrary amount of money, possession of which you may need to demonstrate to customs officials as proof that you can support yourself while in their country. A credit card will often suffice.

Wholesaler / Consolidators who sell tickets only to retail travel agents.

Travel Resources

In preparing to research this book we consulted innumerable travel guides. We found the following guides particularly useful. If you plan to stay in a hub city for more than a few days, or to visit the surrounding area, these guidebooks are among the best available.

The Berkeley Guides are the bold newcomers on the block, finally giving *Let's Go* a bit of competition for the student market. The main difference between the two is the *Berkeley* trend towards covering more outdoor activities, and more ways to get involved, rather than just coming to watch.

Europe Through The Back Door takes you off the well-worn tourist track, and shows you the kinds of places that the locals patronize. Author Rick Steves tracks down family run inns and restaurants that stay in business by offering good value to return customers, rather than gouging tourists.

The Hostel Handbook for the USA and Canada is the most efficient and cost-effective travel guidebook we have ever used. In a quick and to-the-point manner, it provides contact information and prices for almost every hostel in North America. The information is extremely fresh, being updated every spring for the current year's edition. Available at hostels, or by sending a check or money order for $3 (payable to Jim Williams) to 722 Saint Nicholas Avenue, New York, NY 10031, USA.

Let's Go is the classic Europe handbook, and has been the bible for a generation of student travelers. Over the years they have added in-depth regional and country guides to most of Europe and North America.

Lonely Planet guides cover most of the world, with a focus on off-the-beaten-track destinations. In fact, if you can get there only by backpacking in, this is the guidebook you are likely to find there. Their *On a Shoestring* series covers large geographic areas from an ultra-budget perspective, while the *Travel Survival Kits* focus on smaller regions with a greater depth of coverage and wider price range.

Moon Handbooks do a great job of presenting historic and cultural

233

background in a way that is relevant to the here-and-now of the independent traveler. Their practical information on accommodations and sights is highly reliable. We like their map-laden Southeast Asia volume, and look forward to trying out their broad series of guides to the rest of Asia, the Pacific, and North America.

The Native's Guide to New York City covers goings-on in the Big Apple like only a local could. Natives don't need accommodations, so you won't find them reviewed here. But if you are looking for a thousand things to do while in Manhattan (many of them free), author Richard Laermer's book is the one to get.

The Rough Guides dig deeper than most travel books to uncover things that only the hippest locals would know about. Their San Francisco book, for example, is utterly flawless. Every underground club and offbeat activity has been tracked down and accurately described. The down-to-earth and irreverent tone is sure to be appreciated by the independent budget traveler.

Travelers' Tales (O'Reilly and Associates) is a new series which collects the first-hand experiences of some of the world's best travel writers. You won't find hotel and restaurant reviews, but short of living there yourself, there is no better way to get a feel for a country. Current guides cover Thailand, India, and Mexico, with more in the works.

DISCOUNT AIRFARE NEWSLETTERS

Those of you who plan to take more than a few courier flights a year will save a great deal of time and telephone expenses by subscribing to a courier newsletter. The courier newsletters provide updated routes and prices, so you don't have to call each company yourself. For non-courier frequent fliers, we list a source of unpublished fare codes, which let you get in on discounts negotiated by large corporations and conventions. Newsletters seem to come and go, so we have listed some of the most stable players.

Travel Unlimited is the classic courier newsletter. Editor Steve Lantos' periodical has been instilling wanderlust in travelers since 1987. In addition to a monthly update of courier options, *Travel Unlimited* covers the latest trends in general low-budget travel.

Subscriptions run $25 a year. For information and a free sample newsletter, write to PO Box 1058A, Allston, MA 02134, USA.

The International Association of Air Traveler Couriers is the brash, high-tech upstart in the courier newsletter field. They offer members two different bimonthly publications. Odd months **The Air Courier Bulletin** provides updated courier information from most major U.S. cities as well as a few foreign points. Even months, **The Shoestring Traveler** is full of personal travel accounts from the editors and from members. Nifty high-tech features include a 24-hour fax-on-demand information retrieval system (for those who need up-to-the-minute courier flight availability information) and a computer bulletin board, from which you can download articles from past issues, and trade thoughts with other association members. Subscriptions cost $42 a year. Write to PO Box 1349, Lake Worth, FL 33460, USA for an information packet.

Lastly, here is a way for travelers on domestic flights within the USA to get the same discounts that the big corporations and conventions get.

The Travel Confidential Society offers a monthly newsletter outlining all of the airfare, hotel, and car rental discounts available to convention-goers nationwide. You don't necessarily have to attend the convention to get the discount airfare. The newsletter provides the code numbers you need to obtain these "confidential" group rates. Annual dues are $95, which may be deductible for business-people. The listings are extensive, and there is a six month money-back guarantee. For more information on this impressive resource, call ☎ (800) 992 8972.

INDEX

Green Tortoise
Adventure Travel

SLEEPER COACHES
YOSEMITE REDWOODS
ALASKA GRAND CANYON
COAST to COAST
NATIONAL PARKS LOOPS
BAJA COSTA RICA
1-800-TORTOISE (867-8647) or 415-956-7500

How to Order More Books

The Worldwide Guide to Cheap Airfares makes a great gift for budget travelers. There are lots of ways you can order additional copies. First, check at your local bookstore. If they don't have it, you can order by telephone with a credit card. Call 24 hours a day, 365 days a year at ☎ (800) 78 BOOKS. [From outside the USA, call ☎ (510) 276 1532.] You can also complete the order form and fax your order to 510/ 276 1531. Or enclose a check or money order (in U.S. dollars) along with the form and mail it to the address below. Make checks payable to Insider Publications. Each copy costs $14.95 plus shipping ($2.50 for the first book, $1.00 for each additional book), and tax if necessary ($1.23 per book for California residents only).

To encourage you to explore the Internet, we'll knock $2 off the price of each book for all credit card orders placed by e-mail. Just type in the information requested on the order form, and e-mail it to:

insider@sfnet.com.

Mail order form to:

Insider Publications
2124 Kittredge Street, Third Floor
Berkeley, CA 94704 USA

ORDER FORM

NAME

ADDRESS

CITY, STATE, POSTAL CODE, COUNTRY

TELEPHONE

PAYMENT METHOD (CIRCLE ONE)

CHECK   MONEY ORDER   VISA   MASTERCARD   AMEX

CREDIT CARD NUMBER, EXPIRATION DATE

NAME AS IT APPEARS ON THE CREDIT CARD

SIGNATURE OF CARDHOLDER

Please send me:

_____ book(s) @ $14.95 each =	$
Shipping ($2.50 for the first book, $1 for each additional book)	
Tax ($1.23 per book for California residents only)	
Discount for ordering via e-mail (subtract $2 per book)	
TOTAL	$

Credit card orders will be shipped within 24 hours.